First World War
and Army of Occupation
War Diary
France, Belgium and Germany

38 DIVISION
113 Infantry Brigade
Royal Welsh Fusiliers
15th Battalion
1 December 1915 - 28 February 1918

WO95/2556/1

The Naval & Military Press Ltd
www.nmarchive.com
Published in association with The National Archives

Published by

The Naval & Military Press Ltd

Unit 10 Ridgewood Industrial Park,

Uckfield, East Sussex,

TN22 5QE England

Tel: +44 (0) 1825 749494

www.naval-military-press.com

www.nmarchive.com

This diary has been reprinted in facsimile from the original. Any imperfections are inevitably reproduced and the quality may fall short of modern type and cartographic standards.

Contents

Document type	Place/Title	Date From	Date To
Heading	WO95/2556/1		
Heading	15th Bn Roy Welsh Fus. Dec 1915-Feb 1918		
Heading	15th R. Welsh Fus. Vol I Decbr 1915 and Jany 1916		
Heading	War Diary Of 15th Battalion Royal Welsh Fusiliers. From December 1.12.1915 To 8.2.1916		
War Diary	Winchester	01/12/1915	01/12/1915
War Diary	Southampton	01/12/1915	02/12/1915
War Diary	Havre	03/12/1915	03/12/1915
War Diary	Blendecques	04/12/1915	04/12/1915
War Diary	Warke	05/12/1915	19/12/1915
War Diary	La Gorgue	19/12/1915	26/12/1915
War Diary	Merville	27/12/1915	07/01/1916
War Diary	Richebourg St. Vaast	08/01/1916	14/01/1916
War Diary	Locon	15/01/1916	24/01/1916
War Diary	Locon and Richebourg St Vaast	25/01/1916	08/02/1916
War Diary	War Diary Of 15th Battalion R.W.F. From 9.2.16 to 29.2.16 (Volume II)		
War Diary	Locon	09/02/1916	17/02/1916
War Diary	Givenchy	20/02/1916	21/02/1916
War Diary	Gorre	25/02/1916	27/02/1916
War Diary	Givenchy	29/02/1916	29/02/1916
Operation(al) Order(s)	Operation Order No.1	21/02/1916	21/02/1916
Operation(al) Order(s)	Operation Order No.2 By Lieut Colonel. R.C. Bell Comdg.	28/02/1916	28/02/1916
Miscellaneous			
Heading	15 R.W. Fus Vol 3		
Heading	War Diary Of 15th Battn. R.W.F. From 4th March 1916 To 31st March 1916 (Volume 3)		
War Diary	Givenchy	04/03/1916	07/03/1916
War Diary	Hingette	08/03/1916	15/03/1916
War Diary	La Touret	15/03/1916	15/03/1916
War Diary	Festubert	16/03/1916	20/03/1916
War Diary	Le Touret	21/03/1916	21/03/1916
War Diary	Festubert	24/03/1916	24/03/1916
War Diary	Festubert Village	28/03/1916	31/03/1916
War Diary	Amplier	31/03/1916	31/03/1916
Operation(al) Order(s)	Operation Order No. 3 By Lieut Colonel R.C. Bell Commdg. 15th R.W.F.	04/03/1916	04/03/1916
Operation(al) Order(s)	Operation Order No. 4 By Lieut Colonel R.C. Bell Commdg. 15th R.W.F.	07/03/1916	07/03/1916
Operation(al) Order(s)	Operation Order No. 5 By Lieut Colonel R.C. Bell Commdg. 15th R.W.F.	16/03/1916	16/03/1916
Operation(al) Order(s)	Operation Order No. 6 By Lieut Colonel R.C. Bell Commdg. 15th R.W.F.	24/03/1916	24/03/1916
Operation(al) Order(s)	Operation Order No. 7 By Lieut Colonel R.C. Bell Commdg. 15th R.W.F.	30/03/1916	30/03/1916
Heading	War Diary Of 15th Battn. R.W.F. from April 1916 to April 1916 (Volume 4)		
War Diary	Hingette	01/04/1916	08/04/1916
War Diary	Givenchy	09/04/1916	13/04/1916

War Diary	Gorre	13/04/1916	16/04/1916
War Diary	Hingette	16/04/1916	16/04/1916
War Diary	Estaires	17/04/1916	17/04/1916
War Diary	Riez Bailleul	18/04/1916	22/04/1916
War Diary	La Gorgue	24/04/1916	30/04/1916
Operation(al) Order(s)	Operation Order No. 8 By Lieut. Colonel R.C. Bell Commdg 15th Bn. R.W.F.	07/04/1916	07/04/1916
Operation(al) Order(s)	Operation Order No. 9 By Lieut. Colonel R.C. Bell Commdg 15th Bn. R.W.F.	08/04/1916	08/04/1916
Operation(al) Order(s)	Operation Order No. 10 By Lieut. Colonel R.C. Bell Commdg 15th Bn. R.W.F.	15/04/1916	15/04/1916
Operation(al) Order(s)	Operation Order No. 11 By Lieut. Colonel R.C. Bell Commdg 15th Bn. R.W.F.	20/04/1916	20/04/1916
Heading	War Diary Of 15th Battalion R.W.F. (1st London Welsh) from 1st May 1916 to 31st May 1916 (Volume V)		
War Diary	Laventie	01/05/1916	18/05/1916
War Diary	La Gorgue	19/05/1916	31/05/1916
Operation(al) Order(s)	Operation Order No. 12 By Major H. Hodson Comdg 15th Bn. R.W.F.	30/04/1916	30/04/1916
Operation(al) Order(s)	Operation Order No. 13 By Major H. Hodson Comdg 15th Bn. R.W.F.	04/05/1916	04/05/1916
Operation(al) Order(s)	Operation Order No. 14 By Major H. Hodson Comdg. 15th Battn. R.W.F.	06/05/1916	06/05/1916
Miscellaneous	Narrative Of The Raid.		
Miscellaneous	Notes On The Raid		
Operation(al) Order(s)	O.O. 15 By Major Hodson Comdg. 15th Bn. R.W.F.	13/05/1916	13/05/1916
Miscellaneous	O.O. 16 By Major Hodson Comdg. 15th Bn. R.W.F.	16/05/1916	16/05/1916
Operation(al) Order(s)	Operation Order No. 16a By Lieut Colonel R.C. Bell Commdg. 15th Bn R.W.F.	24/05/1916	24/05/1916
Operation(al) Order(s)	Operation Order No. 17 By Lieut Colonel R.C. Bell Commdg. 15th Bn R.W.F.	29/05/1916	29/05/1916
Heading	War Diary Of 15th Battalion R.W.F. From 1st June 1916 To 30th June 1916 Volume VII		
War Diary	Riez Bailleul	01/06/1916	10/06/1916
War Diary	Merville	11/06/1916	11/06/1916
War Diary	Busnettes	12/06/1916	12/06/1916
War Diary	Floringhem	14/06/1916	14/06/1916
War Diary	Bailleul-Aux-Cornailles	15/06/1916	25/06/1916
War Diary	Vacquerie-Le-Boucq	26/06/1916	30/06/1916
Heading	15th Battn. The Royal Welsh Fusiliers. July 1916		
Heading	War Diary Of 15th Battn. R.W.F. (1st London Welsh) From 1st July 1916 To 31st July 1916 (Volume VII)		
War Diary	Puchevillers	01/07/1916	02/07/1916
War Diary	Lealvillers	03/07/1916	03/07/1916
War Diary	Ribemont	04/07/1916	04/07/1916
War Diary	Mametz	05/07/1917	08/07/1917
War Diary	Minden Post	08/07/1916	10/07/1916
War Diary	Mametz Wood	10/07/1916	11/07/1916
War Diary	Ribemont	11/07/1916	11/07/1916
War Diary	Ergnies	12/07/1916	14/07/1916
War Diary	Authie	15/07/1916	17/07/1916
War Diary	Couin	17/07/1916	17/07/1916
War Diary	Coigneux	18/07/1916	24/07/1916
War Diary	Auchonvillers	24/07/1916	28/07/1916
War Diary	Bus-Les-Artois Thievres	29/07/1916	31/07/1916

War Diary	Herzeele	31/07/1916	31/07/1916
Heading	15. Battn. R.W.F. War Diary For August 1916		
Heading	War Diary Of 15th Battn. R.W.F. (London Welsh) From 1st August 1916 To August 31st 1916 Volume VIII		
War Diary	Herzeele	01/08/1916	01/08/1916
War Diary	St. Jan Ter Biezen	02/08/1916	20/08/1916
War Diary	Ypres	20/08/1916	31/08/1916
Heading	War Diary 15th Battalion R.W.F. For September 1916 Vol 9		
War Diary	Ypres	01/09/1916	30/09/1916
Heading	War Diary Of 15th Battalion Royal Welsh Fusiliers. October 1916 Vol 10		
Heading	War Diary Of 15th Battn. R.W.F. From October 1st 1916 To October 31st 1916 Volume X		
War Diary	Elverdinghe-Sector Ypres	01/10/1916	31/10/1916
Miscellaneous	Raid.	20/10/1916	20/10/1916
Miscellaneous	38th Division No. G. S. 498	14/10/1916	14/10/1916
Miscellaneous	Narrative Of Raid Carried Out By 15th Battalion Royal Welsh Fusiliers On The Night Of 13/14th October 1916	14/10/1916	14/10/1916
Heading	War Diary For November 1916 15th Battalion Royal Welsh Fusiliers Vol XI		
Heading	War Diary Of 15th Battn. R.W.F. (London Welsh) From 1st November 1916 To 30 November 1916 Volume XI		
War Diary	Ypres Elverdinghe Sector	01/11/1916	30/11/1916
Heading	15th Battn. Royal Welsh Fusiliers War Diary For December 1916 Vol 12		
Heading	War Diary Of 15th Battalion R.W.F. (London Welsh) From 1st December 1916 To 31st December 1916 Volume XII		
War Diary	Ypres Elverdinghe Sector	01/12/1916	13/12/1916
War Diary	Bollezeele	14/12/1916	31/12/1916
Heading	War Diary For January 1917 15th Battn. Royal Welsh Fusiliers. Vol 13		
Heading	War Diary Of 15th Battalion R W F (London Welsh) From January 1st 1917 To January 31st 1917 Volume XIII		
War Diary		01/01/1917	13/01/1917
War Diary	Ypres Lancashire Farm Sector	14/01/1917	31/01/1917
War Diary		25/11/1916	22/01/1917
Heading	War Diary 15th Battn. R.W.F. February 1917		
Heading	War Diary Of 15th Battalion R.W.F. (London Welsh) From February 1st 1917 To February 28th 1917 Volume XIV		
War Diary	W Of Yser Canal Bank Due E Of Brielen	01/02/1917	28/02/1917
Heading	15th Battn Royal Welsh Fusiliers. War Diary For March 1917 Vol 15		
Heading	War Diary Of 15th Battalion R.W.F. (London Welsh) From March 1st 1917 To March 31st 1917 Volume XV		
War Diary	W Of Yser Canal Bank E. Of Brielen	01/03/1917	10/03/1917
War Diary	E. Camp	10/03/1917	29/03/1917
War Diary	Ypres	31/03/1917	31/03/1917
Heading	15th Battn. Royal Welsh Fusiliers. War Diary For April 1917 Vol 16		

Heading	War Diary Of 15th Battalion R.W.F. (London Welsh) From April 1st 1917 To April 30th 1917 Volume XVI		
War Diary	Ypres E. Canal Bank	01/04/1917	10/04/1917
War Diary	W. Canal Bank	11/04/1917	30/04/1917
Heading	15th Royal Welsh Fusiliers War Diary For May 1917 Vol 17		
Heading	War Diary May 1917 15th Bn Royal Welsh Fus		
War Diary	Canal Bank	01/05/1917	04/05/1917
War Diary	Front Line	05/05/1917	08/05/1917
War Diary	Canal Bank	09/05/1917	14/05/1917
War Diary	Front Line	15/05/1917	16/05/1917
War Diary	Canal Bank	17/05/1917	18/05/1917
War Diary	Z Camp	19/05/1917	19/05/1917
War Diary	Houtkerque	20/05/1917	29/05/1917
War Diary	Ochtezeele	30/05/1917	30/05/1917
War Diary	Tatinghem	31/05/1917	31/05/1917
Heading	15th Batt. Royal Welsh Fusiliers. War Diary For June 1917		
War Diary	Tatinghem	01/06/1917	09/06/1917
War Diary	M Camp	10/06/1917	11/06/1917
War Diary	Canal Bank	12/06/1917	12/06/1917
War Diary	Front Line	13/06/1917	16/06/1917
War Diary	Canal Bank	17/06/1917	20/06/1917
War Diary	Front Line	21/06/1917	23/06/1917
War Diary	Canal Bank	14/06/1917	27/06/1917
War Diary	Transport Lines	28/06/1917	28/06/1917
War Diary	Pradelles	29/06/1917	29/06/1917
War Diary	Flechin	30/06/1917	30/06/1917
Heading	15th Bn Royal Welsh Fusiliers War Diary July 1917		
Heading	War Diary For July 15th Battn Royal Welsh Fus.		
War Diary	Flechin	01/07/1917	15/07/1917
War Diary	Steenbecque	16/07/1917	16/07/1917
War Diary	St. Sylvestre Cappel	17/07/1917	17/07/1917
War Diary	Pb Proven	18/07/1917	18/07/1917
War Diary	St. Sixte Area	19/07/1917	19/07/1917
War Diary	Dublin Camp	20/07/1917	22/07/1917
War Diary	Dublin Camp Canal Bank	23/07/1917	23/07/1917
War Diary	Canal Bank	24/07/1917	28/07/1917
War Diary	Dublin Camp	29/07/1917	31/07/1917
War Diary	Front Line	27/07/1917	27/07/1917
War Diary	Dublin Camp	28/07/1917	29/07/1917
War Diary	Canal Bank	30/07/1917	31/07/1917
War Diary	Bn In Attack	31/07/1917	31/07/1917
Heading	15th Battn Royal Welsh Fusiliers War Diary August 1917 Vol 20		
Heading	War Diary 15th Batt Royal Welsh Fus Aug 1917		
War Diary	Iron Cross	01/08/1917	01/08/1917
War Diary	Green Line	02/08/1917	02/08/1917
War Diary	Steenbeek	03/08/1917	04/08/1917
War Diary	Elverdinghe	05/08/1917	05/08/1917
War Diary	Proven	06/08/1917	18/08/1917
War Diary	Rougell Farm	19/08/1917	19/08/1917
War Diary	Leipsig Farm	20/08/1917	23/08/1917
War Diary	Talana Farm	24/08/1917	26/08/1917
War Diary	Candle Tr	27/08/1917	31/08/1917

Heading	15th Battn. Royal Welsh Fuslrs War Diary For September 1917 Vol 21		
War Diary	Langemarck	01/09/1917	04/09/1917
War Diary	Leipsig Fm	03/09/1917	09/09/1917
War Diary	Leipsig Fm Suez Camp	10/09/1917	10/09/1917
War Diary	Suez Camp	11/09/1917	14/09/1917
War Diary	Ecke	15/09/1917	15/09/1917
War Diary	Morbecque Area	16/09/1917	16/09/1917
War Diary	Estaires	17/09/1917	18/09/1917
War Diary	Erquinghem	18/09/1917	25/09/1917
War Diary	Front Line	26/09/1917	30/09/1917
Heading	15th Battn Royal Welsh Fusiliers War Diary For October 1917 Vol 22		
Heading	War Diary For Oct. 1917 15th Bn Royal Welsh Fus		
War Diary	Bois Grenier	01/10/1917	03/10/1917
War Diary	Artillery Farm	04/10/1917	11/10/1917
War Diary	Bois Grenier	12/10/1917	19/10/1917
War Diary	Artillery Farm	20/10/1917	23/10/1917
War Diary	Bois Grenier	24/10/1917	27/10/1917
War Diary	Artillery Farm	28/10/1917	31/10/1917
Heading	15th Battn. Royal Welsh Fusiliers War Diary For November 1917 Vol 23		
Heading	War Diary November 1917 15th Royal Welsh Fus		
War Diary	Bois Grenier	01/11/1917	04/11/1917
War Diary	Artillery Farm	05/11/1917	08/11/1917
War Diary	Bois Grenier	09/11/1917	12/11/1917
War Diary	Artillery Farm	13/11/1917	16/11/1917
War Diary	Bois Grenier	17/11/1917	20/11/1917
War Diary	Artillery Farm	21/11/1917	24/11/1917
War Diary	Bois Grenier	25/11/1917	28/11/1917
War Diary	Artillery Farm	29/11/1917	29/11/1917
War Diary	Erquinghem	30/11/1917	30/11/1917
Heading	15th Battn Royal Welsh Fusiliers War Diary For December 1917		
Heading	War Diary For Dec. 1917 15th Bn Royal Welsh Fus.		
War Diary	Erquinghem	01/12/1917	02/12/1917
War Diary	Front Line	03/12/1917	06/12/1917
War Diary	Front Line & Support Line	07/12/1917	07/12/1917
War Diary	Support Line	08/12/1917	10/12/1917
War Diary	Front Line	11/12/1917	14/12/1917
War Diary	Erquingham	13/12/1917	20/12/1917
War Diary	Front Line	21/12/1917	31/12/1917
Heading	15th Batt. Royal Welsh Fusiliers War Diary For January 1918 Vol 25		
Heading	War Diary For January 1918 15th Batt. R W F		
War Diary	Bois Grenier (Left Subsector)	01/01/1917	01/01/1917
War Diary	Fleubaix	02/01/1918	05/01/1918
War Diary	Bois Grenier	06/01/1918	10/01/1918
War Diary	Bois Grenier (Centre)	11/01/1918	11/01/1918
War Diary	Bois Grenier	12/01/1918	14/01/1918
War Diary	Sailly	15/01/1918	15/01/1918
War Diary	Le Sart	15/01/1918	31/01/1918
Heading	War Diary 15th Battn. Royal Welsh Fusiliers February 1918 Vol 26		
Heading	War Diary For February 1918 15th Battn Royal Welsh Fusiliers.		

War Diary	Le Sart	01/02/1918	01/02/1918
War Diary	Guarbecque	02/02/1918	02/02/1918
War Diary	Kely	03/02/1918	08/02/1918
War Diary	Amplier Kents	09/02/1918	14/02/1918
War Diary	Guarbecque	14/02/1918	14/02/1918
War Diary	Chappellel Duvelle	15/02/1918	15/02/1918
War Diary	Steenwerck	16/02/1918	28/02/1918

38TH DIVISION
113TH INFY BDE

15TH BN ROY WELCH FUS.

DEC 1915-FEB 1918

DISBANDED.

3

15th R. Welch Fus:

Vol I

Decbr 1915

and

Jany 1916

38

Dec 15

Feb '18

Instructions regarding War Diaries and Intelligence Summaries are contained in F. S. Regs., Part II. and the Staff Manual respectively. Title Pages will be prepared in manuscript.

WAR DIARY
or
INTELLIGENCE SUMMARY
(Erase heading not required.)

Army Form C. 2118

Place	Date	Hour	Summary of Events and Information	Remarks and references to Appendices
			CONFIDENTIAL WAR DIARY of 15th BATTALION ROYAL WELSH FUSILIERS. From December 1. 12. 1915 to 8. 2. 1916.	

1875 Wt. W593/826 1,000,000 4/15 J.B.C. & A. A.D.S.S./Forms/C. 2118.

Instructions regarding War Diaries and Intelligence Summaries are contained in F. S. Regs., Part II. and the Staff Manual respectively. Title Pages will be prepared in manuscript.

WAR DIARY
or
INTELLIGENCE SUMMARY
(Erase heading not required.)

Army Form C. 2118

15th Battalion
Royal Welsh Fusiliers.

Place	Date	Hour	Summary of Events and Information	Remarks and references to Appendices
Winchester	1/12/15.	5.45am	The Battalion left Winchester and marched to Southampton arriving there at 12.30 pm	
Southampton.	1/12/15.		where it stayed until 4.30 pm. 2.12.1915. at which hour embarkation commenced.	
		6.0pm.	Prior to this 133. NCO's and men under Capt Owen, and three other Officers left	
— do —	1/12/15.		Southampton on 1/12/1915 by the "City of Chester". The remainder of the Battalion	
	2/12/15	6.0pm.	left Southampton Dock at 6.0pm. on 2/12/1915 by the "Queen Alexandra" and arrived at Havre 7 hours later.	
Havre.	3/12/15.	7.0am	Battalion disembarked and proceeded to Rest Camp.	
"	"	6.0pm	Battalion, less Capt Allison, Lieut R. C. Wilson, and Lieut W. C. Jones also 125 N.C.O's and men, who were detailed to join the 16th Battalion R.W.F., marched to the station at Havre where it entrained at 10.0pm.	
Blendecques	4/12/15.	6.0pm	The Battalion arrived at Blendecques and marched to the village of Warne, where billets were found and Headquarters established	
Warne	5/12/15.		From December 5th 1915 to 19th December 1915 Battalion under training at Warne	
"	19/12/15	6.45am	Battalion paraded and proceeded by motor transport to La Gorgue where each	
La Gorgue	"		Company of the Battalion was attached to a Battalion of the 1st Guard's Brigade for Instruction:-	
			"A" Company attached to 1st Scots Guards. at Riez Bailleul	
			"B" " " " 3rd Grenadier Guards. — do —	
			"C" " " " 1st Coldstream Guards. at Pont du Hem	
			"D" " " " 2nd Irish Guards. — do —	
			On the evening of the 19th December B & D Coys proceeded to trenches with the respective Battalions to which they were attached. A & C. Coys remained in billets.	

1875 Wt. W593/826 1,000,000 4/15 J.B.C. & A. A.D.S.S./Forms/C. 2118.

VR.

Instructions regarding War Diaries and Intelligence Summaries are contained in F. S. Regs., Part II. and the Staff Manual respectively. Title Pages will be prepared in manuscript.

WAR DIARY
or
INTELLIGENCE SUMMARY
(Erase heading not required.)

Army Form C. 2118

15th Battalion Royal Welsh Fusiliers.

Place	Date	Hour	Summary of Events and Information	Remarks and references to Appendices
La Gorgue	20/12/15.	3.0 pm	"A" and "C" Coys proceed to trenches to relieve "C" and "D" Companies.	
"	22/12/15	3.0 pm	"B" and "C" Coys proceed to trenches to relieve "A" and "B" Coys.	
"	24/12/15	3.0 pm	"A" and "C" Coys proceed to trenches to relieve "C" and "D" Coys.	
"	26/12/15.	9.0 pm	"A" and "C" Coys return from trenches after finishing course of instruction with Brigade of Guards.	
Merville.	27/12/15	12 noon	Battalion paraded and were transported to Merville to billets,	
"	28/12/15.		Battalion under training from 28/12/1915 to 6/1/1916.	
"	7/1/16	8.0 pm	Battalion paraded and marched to Richebourg St. Vaast, where they remained in reserve to 16th Battalion R.W.F. for four days.	
Richebourg St. Vaast.	8/1/16.	10.0 am & 2.0 pm	Heavy shelling of billets by Germans ~~with~~ resulting in seven casualties, in "A" Coy. 2 killed 5 wounded.	
"	10/1/16	4.0 pm	Battalion paraded for trenches to relieve 16th Battalion R.W.F. but owing to heavy shelling by the enemy the Battalion retired to dug-out.	
"	10/1/16.	8.30 pm	Relief complete.	
"	14/1/16.	5.0 pm	9th Battalion R.W.F. relieved this Battalion who proceeded to Locon to billets and rest.	
Locon	15/1/16. to 24/1/16		Battalion in reserve, during which time training was carried out.	
Locon and Richebourg St. Vaast.	25/1/16.	9.30 am	Battalion marched to Richebourg St. Vaast to relieve a Brigade of the 19th Division. 15th Battalion R.W.F. remained in support to the 16th Battn R.W.F. who relieved 9th Battalion R.W.F.	

1875 Wt. W593/826 1,000,000 4/15 J.B.C. & A. A.D.S.S./Forms/C. 2118.

Instructions regarding War Diaries and Intelligence Summaries are contained in F. S. Regs., Part II. and the Staff Manual respectively. Title Pages will be prepared in manuscript.

WAR DIARY
or
INTELLIGENCE SUMMARY
(Erase heading not required.)

Army Form C. 2118

15th Battalion Royal Welsh Fusiliers.

Place	Date	Hour	Summary of Events and Information	Remarks and references to Appendices
Richebourg St Vaast	28/1/16.	5.0pm	Battalion proceeded to trenches to relieve 16th Battalion R.W.F. relief complete 7.30 pm.	
"	30/1/16.		First casualty among the Officers of this Battalion was recorded, Lieut W. P. Hinds 'A' Coy being severely wounded by a sniper at No 2 Post Boars Head which resulted in his death on 2/2/1916.	
"	1/2/16.		Battalion returned to Richebourg St Vaast being relieved by 16th Battalion R.W.F.	
"	4/2/16.	5.0pm	Battalion proceeded again to trenches to relieve 16th Battalion R.W.F.	
"	8/2/16.	6.0pm	Battalion relieved and returned to Locon to billets and rest.	

1875 Wt. W593/826 1,000,000 4/15 J.B.C. & A. A.D.S.S./Forms/C. 2118.

Army Form C. 2118

113

Instructions regarding War Diaries and Intelligence Summaries are contained in F. S. Regs., Part II. and the Staff Manual respectively. Title Pages will be prepared in manuscript.

WAR DIARY
or
INTELLIGENCE SUMMARY

(Erase heading not required.)

Place	Date	Hour	Summary of Events and Information	Remarks and references to Appendices
			Confidential War Diary of 15th Battalion R. W. F. From 9. 2. 16. To. 29. 2. 16. (Volume II)	113th Bde 38th Div. 5 shel

1875 Wt. W593/826 1,000,000 4/15 J.B.C. & A. A.D.S.S./Forms/C. 2118.

Instructions regarding War Diaries and Intelligence Summaries are contained in F. S. Regs., Part II. and the Staff Manual respectively. Title Pages will be prepared in manuscript.

WAR DIARY
or
INTELLIGENCE SUMMARY
(Erase heading not required.)

Army Form C. 2118

15th BATTN R.W.F.

Place	Date	Hour	Summary of Events and Information	Remarks and references to Appendices
LOCON	9.2.16 to 16.2.16		Battalion at Locon in Reserve Billets undergoing Training.	
GIVENCHY	17.2.16		Battalion paraded and marched to GIVENCHY, where it remained in Support to 16th Bn. RWF	
	20.2.16		X Company 17th Bn. Lancashire Fusiliers (Bantams) attached to Battalion for instruction.	
	21.2.16	6.30pm	Battalion relieved 16th Bn. RWF	See Operation Order No1 attd
GORRE	25.2.16	6.30pm	Battalion relieved by 16th Bn. RWF and returned to GORRE.	
	26.2.16		Battn. in reserve at GORRE.	
	27.2.16		X Coy. 17th Lancs. Fus. returned to rest. and W. Coy 15th Bn Cheshire Regt. became attached for instruction.	
GIVENCHY	29.2.16	5.45pm	Battn. relieved 16th Battn. RWF	See O.O. No 2 attached.

Norman Elias
Capt & Adjt
15th R Welsh Fusiliers
1/3/16.

1875 Wt. W593/826 1,000,000 4/15 J.B.C. & A. A.D.S.S./Forms/C. 2118.

Copy No. 2

Operation Order No. 7 21/2/16

Battalion will be releived by 13th R.W.F. tonight and will then relieve 18th R.W.F. in left subsector. Time of relief will ... and on relief by 13th R.W.F.

GUIDES FOR 13th R.W.F. - "C" Coy will be releived by "C" Coy 13th R.W.F. and will have one guide for each Post at end of Communication Trench A.9 d 2.8 at 8.30 p.m. Coy will then proceed to relieve 18th R.W.F. without delay at the GROUSE BUTTS. "A" Coy will be releived by "B"Coy 13th R.W.F. and will supply guides at 13th R.W.F. Headquarters 7 p.m. "B" Coy will be releived by "D" Coy 13th R.W.F. and will supply guides at 13th Battalion Headquarters at 7 p.m. "D" Coy will be releived by "A"Coy 13th R.W.F. and will place a guide in the Communication Trench leading from Front Line to their Area to lead Platoons to their positions

CONTROL POSTS AND GUARDS OF SUPPORT AREA. - These will be releived by 13th R.W.F. in the course of the day.

RELIEF OF 18th R.W.F. - It is essential to make the relief continuous along the whole Front, so O.C.Coys will take care that all Platoons file out as soon as relief is complete. Details of the relief have been arranged between O.C. Coys.

RECEIPTS.- O.C.Coys will take duplicate receipts of Trench Stores and send same to Adjutant before 9.0 a.m. 22nd inst.

TRENCH STRENGTH.- The Trench Strength and Disposition Return should accompany the above.

REPORTS AND RETURNS. - The following Reports will be required daily and should reach Battalion Headquarters at times stated.

3.30 a.m. Situation Return.
7.30 a.m. Tactical Progress Report.
11. 0 a.m. No of S.A.A. Mill's Grenades and Rifle Grenades Expended. 10 a.m. to 10 a.m. daily.
1. 0 p.m. Casualty Return. These must include T.M. Batteries return if operation in the Coy area. These should name the Infantry or Artillery unit to which the T.M. casualty belongs in addition to the designation of the Battery.
5.30 p.m. Situation Report.

The Adjutant hopes that O.C.Coys will assist him in being prompt with these Reports. The times mentioned leave him with only one hour to write his own Report to Brigade.

BOMBERS. - O.C. Coys will each select 1 N.C.O. and 11 Bombers to report to Bombing Officer at Battn. H.Q. 4.0 p.m. Skeleton Order. They will proceed to their new positions at once. Battn. Bombers will also parade.

SNIPERS. - The Sergeant Sniper will report at once to Sniping Officer for arrangements regarding the sniping posts.

SIGNALLERS. - will be rationed by the Coys. in whose areas they are operating. C.S.M's will report daily to O.C. Coy that this has been done.

COOKERS.- These will remain in the Support Area, but must not interfere with the 13th R.W.F.'s cooking arrangements. O.C.Coys should endeavour to issue instructions for cooking in them daily and send carrying parties.

RATIONS.- "A" "B" and "D"Coy Rations will be drawn in road near WINDY CORNER. "C"Coy will be drawn at same place as on previous nights.

OFFICER'S VALISES, BLANKETS AND PACKS. - These will be collected together under Coy arrangements. O.C.Coys will inform Adjutant at where they are in order that G.S.Wagons can be detailed to take them to CORRE tonight. "D" Coy will deposit Valises, Blankets and Packs at Battalion Head Quarters at once. A small loading party 1 N.C.O. and 3 men should be left by each Coy.

RELIEF COMPLETE. - O.C.Coys will report relief of 16th R.W.F. complete without delay as the question of timing is of the utmost importanse.

(Sgd) Thomas Elias.
Captain & Adjutant.

[illegible]1/2/1916.

Hour of issue. 12.30 p.m.

Copy No 1 File.
2 War Diary.
3 "A" Coy.
4 "B" "
5 "C" "
6 "D" "

OPERATION ORDER NO 2 BY LIEUT COLONEL R.C.BELL COMMDG. 15

Copy No. 2 Ref. BETHUNE (Combined Sheet) Ed 6.

Battalion will relieve 18th R.W.F. in the Front Line A sub-sector at GIVENCHY.

"A"Coy and one Platoon "C"Coy on the RIGHT. SCOTTISH TRE[illegible]
"C" Coy (minus one platoon) in Support (CALEDONIAN ROAD AND UPPER CUT) (POPPY REDOUBT)
"B" Coy in the centre (GROUSE-BUTTS)
"D" Coy on the left PRINCES ISLAND (one Platoon)
GEORGE STREET (one Platoon)
LE PLANTIN (two Platoons)

All Coys will move in single file via CROSS ROADS at F 5 B 5.8 and not along Canal Bank. Guides will be at this CROSS ROAD at 6.0 p.m.

ORDER OF RELIEF. -

"A" Coy	will move off	at	5.45 p.m.
"D" "	do		5.55 p.m.
"C" "	do		6.10 p.m.
"B" "	do		6.20 p.m.

Special orders for the relief of Snipers, Bombers, and POPPY REDOUBT has been issued.

RATIONS.- Rations will be carried into the Trenches.

COOKERS.- Cookers will take up position in OLD VILLAGE LINE and will leave GORRE at 9 p.m.

HOT FOOD CONTAINERS. - O.C.Coys will ensure that 2 hot food containers per Coy will be drawn nightly from the Soup Kitchen. The soup will be distributed to the men in the early hours of the morning.

RUM RATION.- O.C.Coys will take steps that the Rum Ration is issued at or before midnight and not in the early hours of the morning.

BLANKETS AND PACKS will be stored in Q.M.Stores. Waterproof Capes Overcoats and Mackintosh Sheets to be taken to the trenches.

REPORTS REQUIRED.

1. Relief complete.
2. Disposition and Strength Return(by midnight on night of relief)

DAILY.

3. 3 a.m. Situation Report.
4. 7 a.m. Tactical Progress Report.
5. 10.30 a.m. Expenditure of S.A.A. and Grenades.
6. 1.0 p.m. Casualty Return.
7. 3 p.m. Situation Report.

The above times represents the hour they should be handed into Company Signal Stations. The Adjutant hopes that all Coy Commanders will assist him by being prompt with these reports.

(Sgd) T.Elias.
Captain & Adjutant.

Field.
28/9/1916.
Issued at 9.30 a.m. 29/9/1916.

No 1 Copy Filed.
No 2 War Diary.
No 3 "A"Coy.
No 4 "B" "
No 5 "C" "
No 6 "D" "
No 7 Transport Officer.
No 8 Quarter Master.

3

15 14

13

16

4

16 13

14

15

2

16 13

15

14

5

15 14

16

13

1

15 14

16

13

15 R.W. Fas

Vol 3

WAR DIARY
or
INTELLIGENCE SUMMARY
(Erase heading not required.)

Army Form C. 2118

Instructions regarding War Diaries and Intelligence Summaries are contained in F. S. Regs., Part II. and the Staff Manual respectively. Title Pages will be prepared in manuscript.

Place	Date	Hour	Summary of Events and Information	Remarks and references to Appendices

CONFIDENTIAL.

WAR DIARY

of

15th. BATTN. R. W. F.

From 4th. MARCH 1916 To. 31st. MARCH 1916

(Volume. 3.)

1875 Wt. W593/826 1,000,000 4/15 J.B.C. & A. A.D.S.S./Forms/C. 2118.

Instructions regarding War Diaries and Intelligence Summaries are contained in F. S. Regs., Part II. and the Staff Manual respectively. Title Pages will be prepared in manuscript.

WAR DIARY
or
INTELLIGENCE SUMMARY
(Erase heading not required.)

Army Form C. 2118

Place	Date	Hour	Summary of Events and Information	Remarks and references to Appendices
Givenchy	4/3/16	6.15 pm	16th Batt. RWF. relieved 15th Bn RWF in Front Line Trenches	See O.O. attached.
"	5/3/16		15th Bn RWF in Support, Old Village Lines.	
"	7/3/16	7.0 pm	Batt. relieved in Givenchy by 15th Bn Welsh Regt. after relief Bn. marched to HINGETTE into Reserve Billets.	
Hingette	8/3/16		Batt. in Reserve Area (Hingette) from March 8th 1916 to 15/3/16 undergoing training.	See O.O attached.
Le Touret	15/3/16	9.50 am	Batt. paraded and marched to LE TOURET (Forward Reserve Area) where it remained for one night. resting.	
"	"			
Festubert	16/3/16	7.0 pm	Batt. relieved 16th Welsh Regiment in O.B.L. and Islands. Festubert	See O.O attached.
"	20/3/16	7.0 pm	Batt. relieved in O.B.L. and Islands by 16th Bn. RWF.	
LE TOURET	21/3/16		Batt. in Reserve (Forward area) resting.	
Festubert	24/3/16	7.30 pm	Batt. relieved 16th Bn. RWF. in O.B.L. and Islands	See O.O attached
Festubert Village	28/3/16 to 31/3/16		Batt. relieved by 16th RWF. in O.B.L. & after relief proceeded to Festubert Village. (Support area)	
Hingette	31/3/16	7.30 pm	Batt. relieved by 15th Welsh Regt. & after relief proceeded to Reserve Area. (Hingette)	See O.O attached.

D. Roberts 2/Lt A/Adj

1875 Wt. W593/826 1,000,000 4/15 J.B.C. & A. A.D.S.S./Forms/C. 2118.

OPERATION ORDER NO 3 BY LIEUT COLONEL R.C.BELL COMMD^{G}. 16th R.W.F.

Copy No. 2 Reference BETHUNE Combined Sheet Ed. 6. 4/3/1916.

Battalion will change placeswith with 16th R.W.F. Operation to commence 6.15 p.m.

6.15 p.m. "A" Coy 16 R.W.F. will relieve "C" Coy 15 R.W.F. CALEDONIAN ROAD.
"C" " " " "D" " " LE PLANTIN.
"B" " " (on relief by "D"Coy 15 R.W.F. LE PLANTIN Support) will move to relieve "A" Coy 15th R.W.F. in Right Front.
"D" " 16 R.W.F. (on relief by "C" Coy 15 R.W.F. in GIVENCHY KEEPS) will move to relieve "B" Coy 15th R.W.F. in GROUSE BUTTS.

The following ~~ps~~ will be relieved at 4 p.m.

BOMBERS. SNIPERS. POPPY REDOUBT. SIGNALLERS.

Companies will on relief take the following positions in OLD VILLAGE LINES.

"A" Coy to Farm by Battn H.Q. A. 14 a 9.6 : Coy H.Q. in Block "A"
"B" Coy to WINDY CORNER.
"C" Coy to GIVENCHY KEEPS.
"D" Coy to LE PLANTIN (Support)

The following Control Posts will be taken over. Parties will meet WINDY CORNER 10 a.m.

"B" Coy.	WESTMINSTER BRIDGE.	1 N.C.O.	3 men
	BLOCK "A"	1 "	3 "
	WINDY CORNER.	1 "	3 "
"A" "	GUM BOOT STORE (WINDY CORNER.)	1 "	4 "
	SOUP KITCHEN.	1 (Sgt Cook)	3 men
"D" "	MARAIS E. (F 3 b 9.3)	1 N.C.O.	3 men.
	LE PLANTIN. (A 8 a 7.8)	1 "	3 "
	GUM BOOT STORE LE PLANTIN.	1 "	2 "

Blankets will be brought up after relief.

(sgd) T.Elias,
Captain & Adjutant.

Issued at 8 p.m. 3/3/16.

Copy No 1. Filed.
do 2 War Diary.
do 3 "A" Coy
do 4 "B" "
do 5 "C" "
do 6 "D" "
do 7 T.O.
do 8 Q.M.

OPERATION ORDER NO 4 BY LIEUT COLONEL R.C.BELL COMMDG. 15th R.W.F.

COPY NO. 2 — REFERENCE BETHUNE COMBINED SHEET ED. 6

Battalion will be relieved by 13th Battalion WELSH REGT in OLD VILLAGE LINE and CONTROL POSTS.

O.C.s "A" and "B" Coys 15th R.W.F. will send one guide per Coy to meet two incoming Companies VAUXHALL BRIDGE 7.30 p.m.

O.C.s "C" and "D" Coys will send one guide per Coy to CROSS ROADS F 5 b 5.2 at 7.0 p.m. to meet two incoming Companies.

Reports that relief is complete should be sent to Battalion H.Q. by both Regiments.

CONTROL POSTS AND STORES are to be relieved today 7/3/16

On relief Battalion will move off under Company arrangements to take over Billets at HINGETTE. Companies will march via X 20 d and X 20 b to X 13 d. Then over the Canal to X 13 a then via LES CHOQUAUX and W 17 central to HINGETTE.

BILLETS. Billets must be left clean both inside and the ground immediately around them as the incoming Brigade will report on their state to the Division.

RECEIPTS. Most carefully compiled receipts are wanted. They will be made out in duplicate on the printed forms recently handed out to Coys. They must include every conceivable article of Trench Store. Other forms are being circulated for KEEPS. Duplicate copies will be handed to Adjutant by 10.0 a.m. 9th inst.,

TRANSPORT. Battalion Transport will take all blankets, Baggage and Cookers from Old V.L. at dusk and it can be clear of GORRE by 9.30 p.m.

BATTALION ORDERS FOR 9th inst. -

Reveille. 7.0 a.m.
Breakfast. 8.30 a.m.

The morning will be spent cleaning up.

O.C. Coys will send 1 N.C.O. per Platoon to Battn H.Q. at 10.30 a.m. to draw brushes and cleaning material which have been bought out of the profits derived from the REGIMENTAL DRY CANTEEN

Orderly Room. 12.15 p.m.

CARE OF ARMS. - The Commanding Officer requires O.C.Coys to hand over a Certificate by 11.0 a.m. 9th inst., that all Rifles have been inspected by an Officer and certified clean. If Rifles are in ~~any~~ every way satisfactory the rest of the day will be devoted exclusively to cleaning up clothes and equipment in Billets. There will be no Parades if there is general satisfaction with the cleanliness of the Battalions Rifles.

(sgd) T.Elias.
Captain & Adjutant.

March 7th 1916.
Issued at 11.15 a7m3/16.
No 1 Copy Filed.
2 " War Diary.
3 " "A"Coy.
4 " "B" "
5 " "C" "
6 " "D" "
7 " T.O.
8 " Q.M.

OPERATION ORDER NO 4 BY LIEUT COLONEL R.C.BELL COMMDG. 15th R.W.F.

COPY NO. 2 REFERENCE BETHUNE COMBINED SHEET ED. 6

Battalion will be relieved by 13th Battalion WELSH REGT in OLD VILLAGE LINE and CONTROL POSTS.

O.C.s "A" and "B" Coys 15th R.W.F. will send one guide per Coy to meet two incoming Companies VAUXHALL BRIDGE 7.30 p.m.

O.C.s "C" and "D" Coys will send one guide per Coy to CROSS ROADS F 5 b 5.2 at 7.0 p.m. to meet two incoming Companies.

Reports that relief is complete should be sent to Battalion H.Q. by both Regiments.

CONTROL POSTS AND STORES are to be relieved today 7/3/16

On relief Battalion will move off under Company arrangements to take over Billets at HINGETTE. Companies will march via X 20 d and X 20 b to X 13 d . Then over the Canal to X 13 a then via LES CHOQUAUX and W 17 central to HINGETTE.

BILLETS. Billets must be left clean both inside and the ground immediately around them as the incoming Brigade will report on their state to the Division.

RECEIPTS. Most carefully compiled receipts are wanted. They will be made out in duplicate on the printed forms recently handed out to Coys. They must include every conceivable article of Trench Store. Other forms are being circulated for KEEPS. Duplicate copies will be handed to Adjutant by 10.0 a.m. 9th inst.,

TRANSPORT. Battalion Transport will take all blankets, Baggage and Cookers from Old V.L. at dusk and it can be clear of GORRE by 9.30 p.m.

BATTALION ORDERS FOR 9th inst. - Reveille. 7.0 a.m.
Breakfast. 8.30 a.m.

The morning will be spent cleaning up.
O.C. Coys will send 1 N.C.O. per Platoon to Battn H.Q. at 10.30 a.m. to draw brushes and cleaning material which have been bought out of the profits derived from the REGIMENTAL DRY CANTEEN

Orderly Room. 12.15 p.m.

CARE OF ARMS. - The Commanding Officer requires O.C.Coys to hand over a Certificate by 11.0 a.m. 9th inst., that all Rifles have been inspected by an Officer and certified clean. If Rifles are in ~~any~~ every way satisfactory the rest of the day will be devoted exclusively to cleaning up clothes and equipment in Billets. There will be no Parades if there is general satisfaction with the cleanliness of the Battalions Rifles.

(sgd) T.Elias.
Captain & Adjutant.

March 7th 1916.
Issued at 11.15 a 7/3/16.
No 1 Copy Filed.
2 " War Diary.
3 " "A" Coy.
4 " "B" "
5 " "C" "
6 " "D" "
7 " T.O.
8 " Q.M.

OPERATION ORDER NO 6 BY LIEUT COLONEL R.C. BELL (Comdg.)

REFERENCE BETHUNE COMBINED SHEET Ed 6. 16/3/16.

COPY NO.

Battalion will relieve 16th WELSH REGIMENT in the right sub sector FESTUBERT 7.0 p.m. tonight. The Battalion will move in the following order each party named below being in receipt of a paper from O.C. Coys of its destination and strength.

"B" COMPANY. Right center O.B.L.

ISLANDS	GUIDES.		STRENGTH.
No 1 & 2.	1		2 N.C.O's 7 men.
No 3 & 4	1		2 " 7 "
No 5 & 6	1		2 " 7 "
No 7 & 8	1		2 " 7 "
Princes Island.	1		2 " 23 "
Stretcher Bearers.			4 "
Signallers.			1 " 2 "
Officer in charge.		1 Off.	
Total.	5	2	11 " 57 "

Remainder of Coy. Right sector O.B.L.

"D" COMPANY. Left Flank O.B.L.

ISLANDS.	GUIDES.		STRENGTH.
No 9	1		2 N.C.O's 7 men.
No 10	1		2 " 7 "
No 11	1		2 " 13 "
No 12	1		2 " 11 "
No 13	1		2 " 7 "
Signallers.			1 2 "
Stretcher Bearers.			4
Officer in Charge.		1 Off.	
	BBB	1 " 1	11 " 51 "

Remainder of Coy. Left Flank O.B.L.

RELIEFS. The relief of the above Islands will be carried out every 48 hours and Rations to be brought up nightly by Coys All Coy Officers should visit their Islands nightly.

"A" COMPANY. The entire Coy will occupy the entire center O.B.L.

"C" COMPANY. GEORGE STREET. One guide 1 Off. 25 O.R.

No 5 Redoubt. " 1 N.C.O. 3 men

Le Plantin. E. 2 " 7 "

Grouse Butts. Remainder of Coy.

TIME OF STARTING. Coys will move off in above order in single file at 5.45 p.m. the Adjutants of the two Battalions will arrange the relief with the guides at Estaminet Corner.

RATIONS. Rations of all Coys will be brought to the end of BARNTON ROAD TRENCH on Limbers. From there they will be losded on Trolleys by "A" "B" and H.Q. Coys and wheeled up to O.B.L. Parties of 6 per Coy should be detailed for this. Similarily all Coy and H.Q. Baggage should be wheeled up to O.B.L. O.C. "C" Coy will detail the usual Ration Party of 25 or 30 men to carry the rations from this poin

WATER. Water Carts will be at Estaminet Corner O.C. Coys are responsible that sufficient jars are filled up nightly and wheeled on trolleys to O.B.L. for carriage to Islands This is most important

PACKS AND BLANKETS. These must be stored at once under Coy arrangements in the Building already selected. Officers are advised to take as little as possible into the line.

in ord r to make use of the trolleys rather than carrying parties at all times.

WORK. A definite scheme of work for each Island and each Trench must be drawn up by O.C. Coys and strictly adhered to. Every man must make a GOOSEBERRY daily. Wire in front of Trenches must also be strengthened by special parties every night.

PATROLS. O.C. Coys are responsible that "NO MAN'S LAND" in front of their sector is patrolled under Coy arrangements nightly without orders from H.Q. Battalion Patrols will also be organised.

BOMBERS. Battalion Bombers will parade under 2/Lt W.M.Morgan in time to reach the O.B.L. at 6.30p.m. where they will be distributed in accordance with the plan adopted by the 16th. Welsh Regiment.
The G.O.C. wishes to state that the equipment of Bombers was too readily thrown aside in the last Section. Their equipment and rifles were often in a dirty condition. Bombers must wear equipment except when required to stand to for instant action.

SNIPERS. Snipers will parade with Bombers under Lieut. R.C.Wilson and will be distributed under 16th Welsh Regiment arrangements until the Sniping Officer considers that a redistribution is necessary. This line offers great opportunities for Snipers as the enemy has been exposing himself a good deal lately.

REPORTS. The following reports will be required:-

No. 1 Relief Complete.
No. 2 Trench Strength.
Daily.
No. 3 3 a.m. Situation Report.
No 4 7 a.m. Daily Progress Report.
No. 5 10 a.m. Ammunition and Grenade Return.
No. 6 1 p.m. Casualty Return.
No. 7 3 p.m. Situation Return.

Salvage. Salvage must be collected energetically and dumped at Railhead O.B.L. "C" Coy. will dump salvage at end of BARNTON TRENCH. All Coys. will send daily list of salvage to H.Q.

SPECIALIST OFFICERS. All specialist Officers will live and mess with their respective Coys. during this tour, as there is no accomodation at H.Q.

(Signed) T.Elias,
Captain & Adjutant.

COPY No. 2

[illegible] No. 6 BY LIEUT COLONEL [illegible] (COMMDG) 15th Bn. R.W.F.

REFERENCE BETHUNE COMBINED SHEET [illegible] [illegible]/[illegible]/16.

Battalion will relieve 15th R.W.F. in RIGHT SUB-SECTOR FESTUBERT 7.30 p.m. tonight.
Coys will parade and move off in following order at [illegible] pm and march via TUNING FORK to meet guides at F.5 b [illegible]

"C" COY. RIGHT GROUP ISLANDS.

ISLANDS.	GUIDES.	STRENGTH.
PRINCES.	1 Off.	[illegible] O.R.
Signallers.		[illegible]
Stretcher Bearers.		[illegible]
ISLANDS. No 1 & 2.		[illegible]
" 3 & 4.		4 O.R.
Signallers.		[illegible] O.R.
Stretcher Bearers.		[illegible]
ISLANDS. 5 & 6.		[illegible]
" 7 & 8.		4 O.R.
		4 O.R.

This Coy will supply [illegible] Sentry Groups [illegible] men each by night to No 1 & 2 [illegible] positions.

Remainder of Coy in RIGHT CENTER O.B.L.

"A" COY. LEFT GROUP ISLANDS.

ISLANDS.	GUIDES.	STRENGTH.
No 9.		4 O.R.
No 10.		4 O.R.
No 10 a		(Evacuated by day)
No 11.		4 O.R.
Signallers.	1 Off.	[illegible] O.R.
Stretcher Bearers.		[illegible]
No 12.		7 O.R.
No 13.		7 O.R.

Remainder of Coy LEFT FLANK. O.B.L.

RELIEFS. Relief of above Islands will be carried out every 24 hours if conditions are bad, but normally every 48 hours.

"D" COY. The entire Coy will occupy centre O.B.L.

"B" COY.

GEORGE STREET.	1 Off.	25 O.R.
No 5 Redoubt.	1 N.C.O.	3 men.
LE PLANTIN. [illegible]	[illegible] "	7 "
VILLAGE GUARD.	1 "	[illegible] "

Remainder of Coy. GROUSE BUTTS.

TRANSPORT. The Transport will arrive at end of BARNTON ROAD TRENCH or in the case of "B" Coy at LE PLANTIN at [illegible] p.m. Coys will make arrangements to send their representatives to draw these.

SANDBAGS. All men proceeding to Islands will carry [illegible] sandbags per man these will be dumped at "A" and "C" Coy H.Q. today.

WORK. O.C. Coys will draw up a written scheme of work for each post under their charge and will send duplicates to Adjt.

PATROLS. Coy Patrols must be organised nightly. Battalion Patrols will be arranged by H.Q.

No 1 Copy Filed. No 5 Copy. C Coy (sgd) T.Elias. Captn & Adjt
2 " War Diary. No 6 " D "
3 " A Coy. 7 T.O.
4 " B " 8 Q.M. Issued at [illegible] a.m. [illegible]/3/16.

OPERATION ORDER NO.7 BY LIEUT.COL.R.C.BELL, COMMANDING 15th. Battn.R.W.F.

COPY NO. 1. 2 ... REFERENCE BETHUNE COMBINED SHEET ED.6

Battalion will be relieved by 15th. Battn. WELSH REGT. in FESTUBERT and RUE DE L'EPINETTE. 31/3/16.

O.C. Coys will send 1 N.C.O. per Coy to be at Road Junction X 16 c at 6.0 p.m. to meet incoming Coys. A.& B. Coys to guides to proceed and return via RUE DE L'EPINETTE AND RUE DU BOIS, C. & D. Coy Guides tomproceed and return via TUNING FORK. O.C. Coys will arrange guides to conduct incoming Coys to Posts Keeps etc held by them at present.

Reports that the relief is complete should be sent tobBattn H.Q. by both Regiments.

On relief Battalion will move off under Coy arrangements to take over Billets at HINGETTE. A. & B. Coys will march via RUE DE LEPINETTE AND RUE DU BOIS to X 16 c . C.& D. Coys will march via TUNING FORK to X 16 c. All Coys will then march via X 15 D. X 21 a to bridge at X 13 d then via LES CHOQUAUX to bridge W. 17 central.

POSTS. The following Posts will be taken over by this Battalion at 10.0 a.m. tomorrow 31 st inst. Guides will be at Road Junction X 20 d 4.7 at 9.0 a.m. to conduct these reliefs to their respective Posts.

"A" Coy will supply:-		1 N.C.O and 3 Men for		CROIX DE FER F. 1 b 5.2
do		1	do	LA HALTE. X 28 c 4.0
"B" Coy	do		do	ESSARS. X 25 a 4.3
	do		do	LONG CORNET. W 23 b 6.1
"C" Coy	do		do	LE HAMEL. X 20 d 7.4
	do		do	LE HAMEL. N.W. X 19 b 8.5
"D" Coy	do		do	LAWE. X 13 c 6.1
	do		do	CHOQUAUX. W 13 a 7.5

Chits will be given to each N.C.O. stating which Post they are to garrison. These Posts will be relieved by 16th R.W.F. on 4/4/16.

BILLETS. Coys will take over same Billets at HINGETTE as previously occupied by them. All Billets in Forward Area must be left clean both inside and the ground immediately around them. Certificates to be obtained from incoming Battalion and sent to Orderly Room by Noon 1/4/16. Reports as to state of Billets at HINGETTE will also be rendered to Orderly Room by Noon 1/4/16.
O.C. Coys will detail 2 men per Coy under Lieut R.V.Jones to hand over Billets to 15th Welsh Regiment. O.C. Coys will also detail 2 men per Coy under Major Edwards to report to Orderly Room at 8.0 a.m. tomorrow to take over Billets from Welsh Regiment at HINGETTE

RECEIPTS. Most carefully compiled receipts are wanted. They will be made out on the printed forms already in O.C. Coys possession. They must include every conceivable article of Trench Stores. Duplicate copies will be handed to the Adjutant by 10.0 a.m. 1/4/16.

TRANSPORT. Battalion Transport will take all Blankets, Baggage, and Cookers from FESTUBERT at dusk. H.Qtrs and "A" Coy baggage will be collected at 2.30 p.m. and dumped at Headquarters Mess at that hour. "D" Coy Baggage will be dumped at ESTAMINET CORNER (F 6 c 4.10) at 2.30 p.m.

Dated 30/3/16. Issued at 3.0 p.m. (sgd) D.Roberts. 2/Lt.
Actg. Adjutant.

Copy No-1. Filed. Copy No 2 War Diary.
" 3 "A" Coy 4 "B" Coy.
" 5 "C" " 6 "D" "
" 7 T.O. 8 Q.M.

Instructions regarding War Diaries and Intelligence Summaries are contained in F. S. Regs., Part II. and the Staff Manual respectively. Title Pages will be prepared in manuscript.

WAR DIARY
or
INTELLIGENCE SUMMARY

(Erase heading not required.)

XXXVIII

Army Form C. 2118

15 Welsh Fus

Vol 4

Place	Date	Hour	Summary of Events and Information	Remarks and references to Appendices

CONFIDENTIAL.

WAR. DIARY.

of

15th BATTN. R.W.F.

From APRIL ~~1914~~ 1916 To APRIL ~~1914~~ 1916

(Volume 4)

5408 8/13

1875 Wt. W593/826 1,000,000 4/15 J.B.C. & A. A.D.S.S./Forms/C. 2118.

Instructions regarding War Diaries and Intelligence Summaries are contained in F. S. Regs., Part II. and the Staff Manual respectively. Title Pages will be prepared in manuscript.

WAR DIARY
or
INTELLIGENCE SUMMARY
(Erase heading not required.)

Army Form C. 2118

Place	Date	Hour	Summary of Events and Information	Remarks and references to Appendices
			Casualties to date. Killed 13 O.R.	
			Died of Wounds 2 Officers	
			10 O.R.	
HINGETTE	April	1-8	Training Wounded 80 O.R.	
GIVENCHY		9	Moved into support, OLD VILLAGE LINE, GIVENCHY, relieving 17th RWF	
		9-13	" " FRONT LINE, Left Sub-sector, relieving 10th S.W.B	
			Casualties 3 O.R. killed; 2 O.R. died of wounds; 19 O.R wounded.	
GORRE		13-16	Moved into reserve at GORRE; relieved by 16th RWF.	
HINGETTE		16	39th Div relieved 38th Div; Battalion relieved at GORRE by 11th Sussex & marched to HINGETTE	
ESTAIRES		17	Battalion marched to ESTAIRES, taking billets of 12th H.L.I	
RIEZ-BAILLEUL		18-20	" " to RIEZ BAILLEUL, relieving 8th N STAFFS in reserve: 38th Div. takes over front of 19th Div at MOATED GRANGE and LAVENTIE	
		20-24	Moved into front line RIGHT SUBSECTOR MOATED GRANGE relieving 16th RWF	
			Casualties	
		22	2Lt WM Morgan wounded	
		"	1 O.R Killed; 1 O.R. wounded	
LA GORGUE		24-30	In Reserve and Training at LA GORGUE: Battalion relieved in trenches on night 24/5 by 10th Welsh Regt from whom it took over billets at La Gorgue	J H Hodson Major 15th R.W.F.

4/19

1875 Wt. W593/826 1,000,000 4/15 J.B.C. & A. A.D.S.S./Forms/C. 2118.

OPERATION ORDER NO 9 BY LIEUT. COLONEL R.C.BELL COMMDG 15th BN. R.W.F.

COPY NO. 2 REF BETHUNE COMBINED SHEET Ed. 6. 7/4/16. 591/b8B

The Battalion will relieve 17th Bn. R.W.F. in Support, VILLAGE LINES, prior to relievigg 11th Bn S.W.B. in Left Sub Sector GIVENCHY, tomorrow morning.

8.15 a.m. Battalion will Parade Head of Column at Battn. H.Q. Route. - Via Pont Avelette. Les Choquaux, Le Hamel, Gorre, and Estaminet Corner where guides will be met.

POSTS. "C" Coy will detail 1. N.C.O. and 3 men for MARAIS. S.W. and "D" Coy will detail half a Platoon for Hilders Redoubt and 50 O.R. for GIVENCHY KEEP.

TRANSPORT. No Transport will be East of GORRE before 9.0 p.m. After that time all movement of Transport to the West will be along the South Bank of the Canal and Vauxhall Bridge Road and all movement to the East via Westminster Bridge Road and the North Bank of the Canal.

Blankets, Packs and Officer Valises will be collected at Coys H.Q. under Coy arrangements and the spot indicated to the Transport Officer for collection. Battalion/baggage will be dumped outside Battn H.Q. H.Q.

All this must be ready by 8.0 a.m. punctually

ADVANCE PARTY. An Advance Party of 2 men per coy plus 1 N.C.O. to to be chosen from "A" Coy will leave HINGETTE at 6.0 a.m. to report at 8.30 a.m. to Battn H.Q. 17th R.W.F. in VAUXHALL BRIDGE ROAD. This party will parade outside Battn H.Q.

SANITARY. Four Sanitary Men per Coy under L/Cpl Ruffel will remain behind after Battalion has moved off for final clear up of Billets. They will come on all together as soon as this has been done and report to Battn H.Q. Captn. L.W.Griffith will also remain behind to hand over Billets and to take Certificates of their cleanliness, and will also come on to Support Area.

BILLETS. On arrival in new Billets O.C.Coys will render a Certificate to Orderly Room as to their cleanliness without delay.

Care must be taken that in advancing from ESTAMINET CORNER that the men keep well into the side of the Road especially if hostile aircraft is sighted.

Sandbags containing private property will be labelled and put with Coy Baggage, and on no account carried on the march

(sgd) N.M.Frost. 2/Lt.
Acting Adjutant.

Issued at 7.45 p.m. 7/4/16.

Copy 1. Filed.
" 2 War Diary.
" 3 "A" Coy.
" 4 "B" "
" 5 "C" "
" 6 "D" "
" 7 T.O.
" 8 Q.M.

OPERATION ORDER NO. 9 BY LIEUT COLONEL R.C.BELL. COMMDG. 15th R.W.F.

COPY NO. REF BETHUNE COMBINED SHEET Ed 6. 8/4/16.

Battalion will relieve 11th Bn. S.W.B. in Left Sub-Section GIVENCHY tomorrow morning 9/4/16.
Battalion Front will extend from Shaftesbury Avenue on the Right to Scottish Trench on the Left. 3 Coys in the Line and one in Support.

5940

<u>LEFT</u>. "C" Coy and 1 Platoon Support Coy ("A")

<u>SUPPORT</u>. "A" Coy minus 1 Platoon.

<u>CENTRE</u>. "B" Coy.

<u>RIGHT</u>. "D" Coy.

Relief will be carried out as follows:-

<u>BOMBERS</u>. O.C. all Coys will detail 2 N.C.O's and 10 men per Coy and the Battalion Bombers to report under Lieut W.M.Morgan to guides at WINDY CORNER at 10.0 a.m. They will relieve Saps and their dispositions will be issued later. They will proceed via HITCHIN ROAD, COLDSTREAM LANE, NEW CUT and WARE ROAD.
An equal number of Bombers will be detailed after 48 hours to relieve the above.

<u>LEFT COY</u>. Will report to guides at WINDY CORNER at 11.0 a.m. and proceed via HITCHIN ROAD, COLDSTREAM ~~ROAD~~ LANE, NEW CUT and WARE ROAD.
One Platoon Support Coy and garrison of POPPY REDOUBT (1 Officer 32 O.R.) who will be under the command of O.C Left Coy, will follow the Left Coy into the Line.

<u>CENTRE COY</u>. Will report to guides WINDY CORNER 11.45 a.m. and proceed via CALEDONIAN ROAD and FRENCH FARM LANE.

<u>RIGHT COY</u>. Will report bottom of QUEENS ROAD 11.30 a.m. and proceed via KINGS ROAD.

The dispositions of Coys in the Line have been arranged between O.C. Coys of the two Battalions.

<u>HELMETS</u>. An issue of Steel Helmets is promised by Brigade before relief.

<u>COOKING ARRANGEMENTS</u>. O.C. Coys will report at once which of the two proposals below they intend to follow.

(1) Cook all food, boil water in the Line.
(2) Support Coy two Platoons of which will be in the VILLAGE LINE to detail carrying Parties to carry hot food and tea from cookers to Coys. This will entail parties to carry tea and bacon for breakfast, dinner at midday and tea in the afternoon. Dry Rations, of course, must be brought into the Line under Coy arrangements nightly.

<u>SOUP KITCHEN</u>. Quarter Master and Coy Q.M.S. will send supply of bones to Soup Kitchen nightly and O.C. Coys must arrange to supply their men with Soup.

<u>REPORTS</u>. The following reports will be required promptly.
Relief complete, ~~Trench~~ Strength and Disposition on taking over.
3.0 a.m. and 3.0 p.m. Situation Report.
10.0 S.A.A. and Grenade expenditure Return.
1.0 p.m. Casualty Return.
7.0 a.m. Work and Tactical Progress.

(sgd) T. Elias. Capt & Ad.

OPERATION ORDER NO 10 BY LIEUT COLONEL R.C.BELL COMMDG 15th BN. R.W.F.

COPY No. 2 Ref. BETHUNE Combined Ed 6. 36 and 36 A. 15/4/16.

59BP

1. Battalion will move to ESTAIRES 16/4/16 prior to taking up a new front South of the LAVANTIE Sector. On 17/4/16 Battalion will go into Reserve at REIZ BAILLEUL.

2. Battalion will Parade at 8.45 a.m. in time to reach the starting point at R 21 D 0.8 10.15 a.m. where it will fall in with the other Battalions of the Brigade. Route will be via LOCON LESTREM, R 4 a, LA GORGUE. The present billets at HINGETTE will be handed over to the 17th Sherwood Foresters. The usual Certificates will be obtained.

3. Captain L.N.V.Evans has been detailed with the Interpreter and 4 N.C.O's to arrange Billets at ESTAIRES. Dinners must be ready for the men on arrival and must therefore be cooking on the march. 1st and 2nd Line Transport, except Lorries which will proceed separately, will accompany the Battalion on the march.

4. On 17/4/16 Battalion will relieve 8th North Staffs of the 57th Infantry Bde., in REIZ BAILLEUL" Coys taking over from their opposite numbers. Battalion will pass PONT LEVIS G 36 c 11.30 a.m. and march via SINT CROIX and M 1 b. An Officer will be detailed to take over these Billets at 8.0 a.m.

MARCH DISCIPLINE. - The Left of the Road will be kept clear at all halts. An Officer will march behind each Company. Uniformity of Dress will be observed in accordance ~~by~~ with arrangements made by ~~with~~ Major Edwards

(sgd) T.Elias.
Captn. & Adjt.

Issued at 4.0 p.m. 15/4/16.

Copy No 1 Filed.
2 War Diary.
3 "A" Coy.
4 "B" "
5 "C" "
6 "D" "
7 T.O.
8 Q.M.

OPERATION ORDER NO 11 BY LIEUT COLONEL R.C.BELL COMMDG. 15th BN. R.W.F.

COPY No. 2   Ref. Map 36.   20/4/16.

1. Battalion will relieve 16th R.W.F. in Right Sub-Section MOATED GRANGE 7.45 p.m. 20/4/16. Guides will be at ROUGE CROIX 7.45 p.m.

2. No movement of Troops in formed bodies larger than a Platoon will take place along the LA BASSEE ROAD.

3. Order of Relief:-

"B" Coy. will take over the SUPPORT AREA the 2 Platoons in ROUGE CROIX E. and ROUGE CROIX W. being relieved prior to the Battalion relief and the Garrisons to proceed to the Support Posts held by 16th R.W.F. under arrangements of O.C. Coy.

"D" Coy. Centre Coy. meet guides ROUGE CROIX 7.45 pm Reilef through ~~SSS~~ TILLEROI Communication Trench.

"A" Coy rendezvous as above. Relief to take place SOUTH SIGN POST LANE or SUNKEN ROAD.

"C" Coy rendezvous as above. Relief to proceed through SOUTH TILLEROI Communication Trench.

TRANSPORT. Rations will be brought to LA BASSEE CROSSING 9.30 p.m. where it will be met by 4 6 men per Coy who will place it on Trolleys for Battalion H.Q. The usual Ration Parties per Coy will be detailed to carry rations to Coy Area from this point.

WATER. Water Carts will not leave the 1st Line Transport. Water Men will proceed to Battn.H.Q. Water will be drawn from Pump by Battn.H.Q. by Water Men and Chlorinated in Tanks. O.C. Coys will use the Hot Food Containers issued to them on 19/4/16 to carry this water to their Areas.

PACKS AND BLANKETS. Packs and Blankets must be collected today and placed in charge of the Q.Master.

(Sgd) T. ELIAS.
Captain & Adjutant.

Issued at. 10.0 a.m. 20/4/16.

Copy No 1 Filed.
" 2 War Diary.
" 3 "A" Coy.
" 4 "B" "
" 5 "C" "
" 6 "D" "
" 7 T.O.
" 8 Q.M.

Instructions regarding War Diaries and Intelligence Summaries are contained in F. S. Regs., Part II. and the Staff Manual respectively. Title Pages will be prepared in manuscript.

WAR DIARY
or
INTELLIGENCE SUMMARY
(Erase heading not required.)

Army Form C. 2118

15th R Welsh Fus
Vol 5

Place	Date	Hour	Summary of Events and Information	Remarks and references to Appendices
			CONFIDENTIAL	XXXVIII
			WAR DIARY	
			OF	
			15th BATTALION. R.W.F.	
			(1st London Welsh)	
			From 1st MAY 1916 To 31st MAY 1916	
			(Volume V)	

1875 Wt. W593/826 1,000,000 4/15 J.B.C. & A. A.D.S.S./Forms/C. 2118.

Instructions regarding War Diaries and Intelligence Summaries are contained in F. S. Regs., Part II. and the Staff Manual respectively. Title Pages will be prepared in manuscript.

WAR DIARY
or
INTELLIGENCE SUMMARY
(Erase heading not required.)

Army Form C. 2118

Place	Date	Hour	Summary of Events and Information	Remarks and references to Appendices
LAVENTIE	1st May.	8 pm	Relieved 16th RWF in support at Laventie (see O.O attached)	O.O 12
	2	"	Laventie support.	
	3	"	" "	
	4	"	" 1. O.R wounded	
	5	"	Moved to front line trenches, FAUQUISSART, relieving 16th RWF. ~~1 O.R wounded~~ (O.O. attached)	OO 13
	6	"	In Front Line 1. O.R. wounded.	
	7	"	Raided enemy trenches. (Operation Order & casualties attached) Raid 11.30 pm - 2.40 a.m 7/8 May. 1. O.R wounded who was not in Raiding party	O.O. 14
	8	"	In front line 1. OR killed 1. OR wounded.	
	9 "	9 pm	Relieved by 16th RWF. Returned to Laventie.	
	10		At Laventie	
	11		"	
	12		"	
	13	" 8 pm	Relieved 16th RWF in front line Fauquissart: Captured German Prisoner from 16th Bavarian Res: Regt - Carl Hanssler of Munich: 1 O.R. killed	OO 15
	14		In front line 1. O.R wounded.	
	15th	"	Three hours bombardment of enemy's trenches. TMB's & Rifle grenades cooperating: our casualties 1. OR wounded	
	16	"	Three hours bombardment of our trenches by enemy in retaliation for our previous day's bombardment Our casualties NIL.	
	17	"	Relieved by 13th Welsh Regt: relief shelled heavily by enemy: our casualties NIL.	OO 16
La Gorgue	18	"	In Divisional Reserve at LA GORGUE	
	19	"	" " . G.O.C in C British Forces in France awards honours for Raid on enemy's trenches 7/8 May.	

R. C. Bell. Lt Col.
Comdg. 15th R.W.F.

5976

1875 Wt. W593/826 1,000,000 4/15 J.B.C. & A. A.D.S.S./Forms/C. 2118.

Army Form C. 2118

WAR DIARY
or
INTELLIGENCE SUMMARY

(Erase heading not required.)

Instructions regarding War Diaries and Intelligence Summaries are contained in F. S. Regs., Part II. and the Staff Manual respectively. Title Pages will be prepared in manuscript.

Place	Date	Hour	Summary of Events and Information	Remarks and references to Appendices
La Gorgue	19	Contd.	D.S.O to Capt Goronwy Owen	
			D.C.M. 22273 Cpl D.W. Bloor	
			" " 22770 Pte P.F. Witten	
			" " 22289 Pte J. Heeson	
			Military Medal } 22329 Sergt G.P. Jones	
			22183 Cpl F.J. Rosser	
			21813 Pte F. Langdon	
			22607 Pte I. Downes	
"	20	May	At La Gorgue training	
"	21	"	" . 2nd Lt W.M. Morgan is awarded Albert Medal (2nd Class) by His Majesty the King for picking up & throwing away a live grenade during grenade instruction, having to grope for grenade in the mud, thus saving several lives	
"	22		At La Gorgue training	
"	23	"	"	
"	24	"		
"	25		Relieved 16th Welsh Regt in Rt Sub Section Front Line Moated Grange: billets at La Gorgue handed over to 11th S.W. Borderers	0016a
"	26		In Front Line 1.O.R Killed	
"	27		" 1 O R wounded	
"	28		" Relieved by 16th Bn RWF	
"	29		"	
"	30		In support at RIEZ BAILLEUL.	
"	31			

R. C. Bell. Lt Col.
Comdg. 15th R.W.F.

0017

1875 Wt. W593/826 1,000,000 4/15 J.B.C. & A. A.D.S.S./Forms/C. 2118.

OPERATION ORDER NO 12 BY MAJOR H.HODSON COMMDG 15th BN R.W.F. FOR 1/5/16.

COPY NO. 2 REFERENCE 36 and 36 A. dated 30/4/16.

1. The Battalion will move into Support at LAVENTIE relieving 16th R.W.F. Billets at LA GORGUE will be handed over to 11th S.W.B.

2. The Battalion will move off from Parade Ground at 6.50 p.m. and will pass the starting point, Railway Crossing L 35 b at 7.5 p.m.

3. 1st and 2nd Line Transport will accompany Battalion. 10 G.S. wagons will arrive in this Area at 4.0 p.m. for loading baggage.

4. Major Edwards will proceed to LAVENTIE in the afternoon to take over from 16th R.W.F. Lieut Wilson will remain behind at LA GORGUE until these Billets are taken over by 11th S.W.B.

5. The following Posts will be taken over by Companies. Garrisons to report to H.Q. 16th R.W.F. LAVENTIE 6.30 p.m.

"A" Coy.	HOUGOUMONT.	1 Platoon	(1 Off. 30 O.R.)
"B" "	PICANTIN.	ditto	ditto
"C" "	LAVENTIE.	2 Platoons	(2 Off. 60 O.R.)
"D" "	DEAD END.	1 Platoon.	(1 Off 30 O.R.)

6. Relief will be reported complete and all receipts taken. Particular care must be exercised in signing for Maps.

Issued at 6.15 p.m. 30/4/16.

Copy No 1 Filed.
" 2 War Diary.
" 3 "A" Coy.
" 4 "B" "
" 5 "C" "
" 6 "D" "
" 7 T. O.
" 8 Q.M.

(Sgd) T. ELIAS.
Captain & Adjutant.
15th Battalion R.W.F.

OPERATION ORDER NO. 13 BY MAJOR HODSON COMMDG. 15th R.W.F. FOR 5/5/16.

COPY NO. 2 REF. MAP.36a BELGIUM AND FRANCE. 6008

1. Battalion will relieve 16th R.W.F. Left Section FARQUISSART 8.0 p.m. 5/5/16. Guides will meet Coys; Cross Roads Laventie East M. 5 b 4.1.7.45 p.m.

2. The following Posts will be taken over by Coys, guides to meet Garrisons 5.30 p.m. at M 6 d 5.4.

"A" Coy.	FIREWORKS POST.	1 Section and 6 Bombers.
"C" "	FLANK POST.	1 Officer ~~35 O.R.~~ 35 O.R.
"D" "	A. I.POST.	1 " ~~35 O.R.~~ 35 O.R.

3. O.C. Coys will detail a runner to direct Garrisons of Posts already held to fall in with the remainder of their Coys on the way to the relief. 1 N.C.O. will remain behind in each Post to hand over and take receipts.

4. Order of Relief.

"A" Coy.	via Dead End Road, Dead End Post, Rotten Row.
"B" "	via Great North Road, Rifleman's Avenue.
"C" "	via do Picantin Avenue.
"D" "	via Picadilly and Bond Street.

RATIONS. Ration Limbers will be on RUE BACQUEROT 9.30 p.m. O.C. two right Coys will detail 1 N.C.O. and 6 men each to push them on Trolleys to RUE TILLELOY where Coy Ration Parties should meet them nightly. O.C. left Coys will detail similar Parties for the left railway, together with the carrying parties from RUE TILLELOY.

R.E.MATERIAL. Coys will indent on Adjutant who will forward indent for Battalion to the Transport Officer. The Transport Officer will take the indent to 151 R.E. every afternoon and will detail two horses to take G.S. wagon with these stores to Battn H.Q. with the Ration Limbers nightly.

SIGNALS. Battalion Runner will stand in the GREAT NORTH ROAD by RUE TILLELOY 7.0 - 7.15 a.m. daily to take Coy Tactical Progress Reports.

Messages to and from Trenches must be by runner when containing anything of a secret nature.

PACKS AND BLANKETS. O.C. Coys will make arrangements to store Packs and Blankets.

(sgd) T.ELIAS.
Captain & Adjutant.
15th Battalion R. W. F.

Issued at 6.45 p.m. 4/5/16.
Copy No 1 Filed.
" 2 War Diary.
" 3 "A" Coy.
" 4 "B" "
" 5 "C" "
" 6 "D" "
" 7 T.O.
" 8 Q.M.

SECRET.

OPERATION ORDER NO 14 BY MAJOR H.HODSON COMMDG. 15th BATTN. R.W.F.
(1st LONDON WELSH)

COPY NO. 2.

6014

MAP REFERENCE. Sheet 36 S.W. 1 Brigade Trench Map Area "K"
Scale 1/10,000

INTENTION. Captain G.Owen assisted by 2nd Lieut N.O.Jones, 2nd Lieut H.Taggart and 2nd Lieut D.F.Ingledon (119th Brigade R.F.A.) with 51 N.C.O's and men will Raid enemy's trenches at N 14 a 7.4.
Operation to commence at midnight 7/8th May 1916.

OBJECT.

1. To kill Germans.
2. To take Prisoners.
3. To capture or destroy Machine Guns.
4. To secure samples of German Equipment, Steel Helmets, Respirators, Ammunition etc.

PRELIMINARY RECONNAISSANCE. At 10.30 p.m. Cpl. Bloor and 4 men will reconnoitre to enemy wire in front of objective: will cut wire where necessary and will return to report on enemy's vigilance.

DISTRIBUTION. The Rading Party will be drawn up at 11.30 p.m. and will leave our Trench at N 14 a ~~8.4~~ 2½.5½. It will proceed along the line of Willows to enemy's wire As a distinguishing mark all faces and hands will be blackened. It will be composed of Right Party under 2nd Lieut N.O.Jones and 20 O.R. Left Party under 2nd Lieut H.Taggart and 20 O.R. and the O.C.Raiding Party (in support) with 11 O.R.

Left and Right Parties will advance side by side in single file led by two Officers.

On reaching point of entry at N 14 a 7.4 Right Party will operate to right for 50 yards, Left Party to left for 50 yards along enemy's trench.

Captain Owen's Party will remain at enemy parapet N 14 a 7.4 and will:-

1. Establish and retain communication.
2. Mark enemy trench at point of entry to right and left Raiding Parties with square of white calico.
3. Widen path through enemy wire for withdrawal.
4. Help with Prisoners and Wounded.
5. Signal to Artillery to barrage (if required).
6. Withdraw when Right and Left Raiding Parties are clear of enemy trenches.

Operation will last for 15 minutes from the time of entry. Three long blasts on the whistle will be the signal for withdrawal.

DISPOSITION OF PARTIES.

Right Party.

2nd Lieut N.O.Jones.
Sergt.O.Gibbs.
2 men with Revolvers and Bludgeons.
3 Grenadiers with Bludgeons, each carrying 12 Grenades.
3 Carriers with Bludgeons each carrying 12 Grenades.
8 men with Bludgeons each carrying 12 Grenades who will block and hold Communication Trenches.
2 men to search dug-outs (one with Revolver, Bludgeon and ~~12 Gre~~ 6 Grenades) (one with Bludgeon and 12 Grenades)
2 men with Revolver and Bludgeon to escort Prisoners)

Left Party.

2nd Lieut H.Taggart.
Sergt G.P.Jones.
2 men with Revolvers and Bludgeons.
3 Grenadiers with Bludgeons each carrying 12 Grenades.
3 Carriers with Bludgeons each carrying 12 Grenades.
8 men with Bludgeons each carrying 12 Grenades who will block and hold Communication Trenches.
2 men to search dug-outs. (one with Revolver, Bludgeon, and 6 Grenades) (one with Bludgeon and 12 Grenades)
2 men with Revolver and Bludgeon to escort Prisoners)

Captain Owen's Party.

Captain Owen and C.S.M. J.Bradshaw.
2 Telephone Operators. R.F.A.
5 men - Wire Cutting Party under Cpl, Bloor.
3 Runners.

CO-OPERATION.

1. Artillery. Will be attached to this Operation Order when arranged with Officer Commanding Left Group 38th Divisional Artillery.
2. M.M.Gs will open frequent bursts of indirect fire over the zone of Operations before and during the raid.
3. Lewis Guns. B.M.G.Officer has arranged to Traverse with Lewis Guns the enemy parapet from points at 60 yards distance from N 14 a 7.4 Left and Right. Lewis Guns will traverse outwards from this point during Operation and withdrawal.

COMMUNICATION.

1. 2nd Lieut Ingledon R.F.A. will be in telephonic communication with Company Headquarters near N 14 a 2½.3½ : Communication thence to Battalion Headquarters and Batteries has been arranged.
2. Failing (1) lamp with Captain Owen's Party will signal with one Red Flash if barrage is required
3. There will be three runners to communicate with Company Headquarters in the Line failing (1) and (2)

REGIMENTAL AID POST. Medical Officer and Orderlies will be at Emergency Dressing Station PICANTIN TRENCH. N.7 d 9½.7 Medical Officer from 130th Field Ambulance will be at Dressing Station Battalion Headquarters with Orderlies and Motor Ambulance.

Captain & Adjutant.
15th Battalion Royal Welsh Fusiliers.

Issued at 8.0 p.m. at M. 6 d 2½.1 6/5/16.
Copy No 1 Filed.
do 2 War Diary.
do 3 O.C.Raid.
do 4 Medical Officer.
do 5 }
do 6 }
do 7 } 113th Infantry Brigade.
do 8 }
do 9 }
do 10 }
do 11 O.C.Left Group 38th Div.Artillery.
do 12 1st Australian Infantry Bde.

NARRATIVE OF THE RAID.

6046

10.45 p.m. Corpl Bloor and 4 men set out on preliminary reconnaissance, with orders also to cut the wire. No message was received from this patrol until 12.30 a.m.

11.30 p.m. Right and Left Raiding Parties drawn up in our trench ready to file out.

12 midnight. No message from preliminary patrol.

12.30 a.m. Runner from patrol reported that an enemy Wiring Party 12 to 15 strong was at work on wire near N 14 a 7.4 the point chosen as the objective of the Raid. Cpl Bloor and 3 men were keeping this party under observation.

12.40 a.m. O.C. Raid decided, after consulting Battalion Headquarters, to lead his parties along line of Willows to a ditch which ran about 40 yards in front of German wire, hoping to better appreciate the situation and, if necessary, to rush the enemy wiring party.

Raiders then filed out and leading files reached the ditch, N 14 a 5.4. O.C.Raid and Sergeant Major advanced alone from this point and met Cpl.Bloor creeping towards line with white tape which he was in the act of laying from the gap in the enemy wire to the ditch. The Cpl. explained that since the departure of his messenger the enemy wiring party had reentered the trenches, and he and his men had gone forward and had cut outer wire. O.C.Raid advanced to the wire and discovered it to be 15 feet wide and the gap to be incomplete. He worked alone for approximately a quarter of an hour, cutting the last ~~feet~~ few feet. There was dead silence around him except the tread of a German sentry in a bay opposite him, having finished, he approached the German parapet across a narrow ditch with a muddy bed. The German parapet was on the far side of this. The sentry at this time was fortunately walking in the fairway of the trench, and not on the fire step. O.C.Raid secured a view of this bay and of the bays to right and left. He estimated that there were 20 men in these three bays standing about in groups, some without equipment and arms.

O.C.Raid then returned to his parties. He fixed a position for the R.F.A. Officer and his two telephonists in a shell hole, and handed over his red flash lamp. He then led his party through the wire.

1.50 a.m. The order to attack was given. 2/Lt H.Taggart sprung forward and shot the sentry dead, and 2/Lt N.O.Jones emptied his revolver into the bay. Another sentry was bludgeoned. This was followed by a shower of bombs into the three bays at the point of entry, putting the 20 men, estimated to be in them, out of action. Both raiding parties secured a foothold in the trench. Two blasts on a hooter then sounded the alarm in the enemy trench.

Right and Left Parties filed into action. Both were suprised at the number of the enemy in adjacent bays and along the traffic way. The Germans stood sandwiched together, some without equipment and arms which seems to show that they did not constitute the ordinary garrison of the trench,

607½

ENEMY EQUIPMENT. Most of the enemy were unarmed and without equipment, they may, therefore, have been miners. They wore Forage caps. Colour of Caps and Uniform was not eaisly distinguishable, but appeared to be Greyish Blue.

It was not possible to capture samples of equipment, arms, ammunition etc, because there was none to be found. The search parties which had been detailed could only operate in a limited area and for a few minutes only.

CO-OPERATION.

1. Machine Guns. No 5 M.M.G.Battery fires 20,000 rounds. This fire was found most useful in distracting attention and preventing the enemy from looking over the parapet during the advance.

   Front line Lewis Guns traversed the parapets on both flanks during the raid.

2. Artillery. Barrage was not signalled. The R.F.A. Officer lost touch with the Raid leader during the operations.

(sgd) R.C.BELL.
Lieut.Colonel.
Commdg. 15th Battn. R.W.F.
(1st London Welsh)

6064

NOTES ON THE RAID.

The enemy were suprised when crowded in his trench during a working party relief of some kind - perhaps the wiring party seen by the preliminary patrol. The presence of so many impeded movement on both sides and accounts for the inability of the raiders to penetrate more than 50 yards of the enemy trench.

METHOD OF ATTACK. On account of the slow progress of the leading Bombers the situation produced the following method of attack :-

Bays were bombed from the ditch outside the parapets by flankers working as advanced parties to the bombers operating round the traverses. This overcame much of the opposition which would otherwise have been met inside the trenches.

WITHDRAWAL. These flankers covered the retirement of the Right and Left Parties from the trenches. They continued to engage and hold up the advancing enemy until all were through the German wire.

ENEMY'S COUNTER METHODS. The enemy had no time to produce or organize a counter attack and the Communication Trenches were blocked with men attempting to get away.

The raiding party was subject to Rifle fire from the Support trenches which were mostly high. Heavy M.G.Fire was opened when the retirement commenced - 6 Machine Guns being counted in action.

EQUIPMENT AND ARMS. The raiding party was equipped as laid down in the Operation order.

1. Bludgeons were extremely useful. They were the helves of entrenching tools with loaded ends.

2. Revolvers were invaluable as they enabled individual Raiders to deal quickly with parties of the enemy where a bomb meant loss of time, and a Bludgeon could not be used.

3. Bombs. The pins were well greased and the detonators carefully examined. They were carried in canvas buckets painted grey and slung over the shoulder. The rims of the buckets were stiffened. Over 200 bombs were used.

ENEMY TRENCHES. These were deep and dug in. Sides of the trenches were almost perpendicular. Floors and sides being boarded. Traverses had rounded corners and were smaller than ours. Length of Bays was about 6 yards. Parados was low.

Men in Support trench were able to sweep "No Man's Land" over the front trench. There were no dug-outs in the area covered. One machine Gun emplacement was found which had neither Garrison nor Machine Gun. Trenches were perfectly dry.

SENTRIES. These were posted singly at intervals of 30 to 40 yards. Sentry bays contained sentry boxes and the sentry walked backwards and forwards along the fire step.

ENEMY WORK. O.C.Raid is of opinion that Mining Operations are in progress opposite N 14 a 7.4 - judging by the number of blue sand bags in the vicinity. He also discovered three thick cables on insulators which he considers are used in conjunction with the mine.

60/b

Although they could offer no opposition, they blocked the way of the bombers. Realizing that there was a delay some bombers on the parapet started to bomb successive bays to right and to left from the ditch outside the parapet. In this way they helped to clear out the bays in front of the bombers who were in the trenches, bombing around the traverses. Right party encountered a narrow communication trench also congested with Germand. The enemy in this trench were vigorously bombed and his casualties were severe. Bombs were thrown as far as possible down the closely packed trench. This heavy bombing prevented the enemy reinforcing through this trench.

Left party also found progress slow on account of the density of the enemy. At one point a general rush was made by the occupants of the ~~trench~~ bay to a bomb store, but before they could secure ~~any~~ bombs they were anticipated and put out of action by our leading bombers. Numerous attempts to gain this Store by the enemy were prevented by steady bombing. Enemy casualties were heavy here.

After 13 minutes of energetic clearing the raiders had secured 50 yards of trench. O.C.Raids then decided to withdraw.

2.10 a.m. The last bombs were thrown from the ditch by the Rear Guard of both parties as they retired through the wire. These bombs fell among advancing Germans and held them up for some minutes.

During this operation neither of the Raiding Parties had suffered a single casualty. O.C.Raid alone sustained a flesh wound from a bomb splinter on his cheek.

WITHDRAWAL. When the parties were reported out of the trench O.C. Raid withdrew. Intense M.G.Fire from the flanks was opened on our men as they retired. Rifle fire was opened from a Support Trench. 2/Lt Taggart was wounded in the back when moving towards the ditch. Capt. Owen carried him across the ditch and sent Sergt. Jones forward for further assistance. Sergt. Jones was wounded as he went away, and fearing he would be cut off, was forced to abandon 2/Lt Taggart, who seemed to have lost the use of his legs. Four search parties failed to locate 2/Lt Taggart.

2/Lt N.O.Jones was seen to fall as he stood on the enemy parapet directing the retirement of his party.

2.40 a.m. Raiding Parties were back in our trench. At this time it was getting too light for further operations.

OUR CASUALTIES.

Captain G.Owen. Slightly wounded (at duty)
2nd Lieut N.O.Jones. Wounded and Missing.
2nd Lieut H.Taggart. Wounded and Missing.
3 O.R. Killed.
1 O.R. Missing.
8 O.R. Wounded (5 slightly)
1 O.R. Wounded (at duty)

ENEMY CASUALTIES. Captain Owen after careful cross examination of hid men places these at 50 killed and wounded. This is a conservative estimate.

(sgd) R.C. BELL.
Lieut Colonel.
Commanding 15th Battalion Royal Welsh Fusiliers.

O.O. 15 By Major Hodson Commdg. 15th Bn.R.W.F.
Copy No. 2. Map Ref. Bde. Trench "K" 13/5/16.
Sheet 36.

1. Battalion will relieve 16th R.W.F. in Front Line Left Sub section ~~SARKUI~~ FAUQUISSART 8.0 p.m. 13th May. Coys will pass Laventie East 7.45 p.m.

2. Order of Relief:- "C" Coy Left. "D" Coy Right.
"B" " Left Centre.
"A" " Right Centre.
No guides will be supplied.

3. The following Posts will be taken over by 5.30 p.m. "C" Coy - AI Post. 1 Off. 35 O.R.
"B" " - Flank. ditto.
"D" " - Fireworks. ditto. and
Battalion Bombers.

4. Rations will be carried. Transport ~~Pass-word~~ for Officers Mess baggage will be at Railheads 9.30 p.m.
Usual carrying parties will be detailed.

Issued at 10.0 a.m. (sgd) T.ELIAS.
Captain & Adjutant.

Copy No 1 filed.
" 2 War Diary.
" 3 "A" Coy.
" 4 "B" "
" 5 "C" "
" 6 "D" "
" 7 T.O.
" 8 Q"M.

O.O. 16 BY MAJOR HODSON COMMDG 15th BN R.W.F.
Copy No. 2 Ref. Sheet 36 16/5/1916.

6092

1. The Battalion will be relieved by 13th Welsh Regiment 8.0 p.m. 17.5.16.

2. Companies will supply following guides:- who will meet the relief at M 5 d 8.7 8.0 p.m.
Fireworks Post, guide to rendezvous 5.30 p.m.
AI and Flank. ditto.
"D" Coy. 1 guide 8.0 p.m. rendezvous as above.
"A" "B" C" Coys ditto.
Relief will be conducted from Left to Right, and guides will look for incoming Coys in that order.

3. On relief Coys will march to LA GORGUE via G 33 d G 32 a L 35 b to take over same billets as previously occupied.

4. Receipts of all Stores must be carefully compiled. All Trench Maps to be handed over.

5. Officers Mess must be at Battalion H.Q. 7.30 p.m. Coy Officer's Chargers will be near Laventie/E Post 10.30 p.m.

Issued at 11.30 a.m. (sgd) T. ELIAS.
Capt Adj

No 1 Filed.
2 War Diary.
3 "A" Coy.
4 "B" "
5 "C" "
6 "D" "
7 T.O.
8 Q.M.

OPERATION ORDER NO 16a BY LIEUT COLONEL R.C.BELL COMMDG 15th BN R.W.F.

COPY NO. 2   Map Ref. Sheet 36 and 36A.   Dated 24/5/16 for 25/5/16.

No 1. The 113th Infantry Brigade will relieve the 115th Infantry Brigade in the MOATED GRANGE SECTION On 25/5/16.

No 2. The 15th Battalion R.W.F. will relieve the 16th Battn. Welsh Regiment in the Right Sub-Section. Moated Grange Section.

No 3. All movements of troops along or East of the BELLE CROIX - LA BASSEE ROAD will be by platoons at 100 yards interval - by day and 50 yards interval at night. Wagons will move by threes at the same intervals.

No 4. **GUIDES.** Guides will be at PONT DU HEM at 8.0 p.m. for each Platoon.

No 5. **PARADE.** The Battalion will parade 6.30 in the following order and will proceed via Road Junction ~~35 b 8.4- 0.5.~~ M 8 b to PONT DU HEM.

"B" Coy.
"C" "
"D" "
"A" "

(Battn will pass Road Junction L 35 b 0.5 at 7.0 p.m.)

No 6. **DISPOSITION OF COYS.** Left "B" Coy. Right "C" Coy. Centre. "D" Coy. Reserve "A" Coy.
Relief will be conducted via Rugby Road.

No 7. **RATIONS.** - Coy Q.M.S. will have rations ready to be picked up by their respective Coys at 7.30 p.m. at PONT DU HEM.
During remainder of tour in Front Line a party of 6 men per Coy will be detailed to report at LA BASSEE CROSSING at 8.45 p.m. for the purpose of pushing trolleys tp Rail head where they will be met by usual ration party from each Coy at 9.0 p.m.

No 8. **TRANSPORT.** Blankets and Packs will be collected at 8.30 a.m. also Q.M. Stores. Officers Valises will be ready for loading at 10.0 a.m. Coy Mess Boxes will be collected at 5.30 p.m.

No 9. **SPECIALISTS.** The following parties will Parade at the undermentioned hours.

Snipers.	1.30 p.m.
Signallers.	1.30 p.m.
Machine Gunners.	1.30 p.m.

Bombers will parade in time to carry out relief at 7.0 p.m.
Men detailed for Patrols will parade with Snipers etc at 1.30.

No 10. **WATER.** Water Carts will not leave the 1st line Transport. Water men will proceed to Battn H.Q. Water will be drawn from pump at Battn H.Q. and Chlorinated in Tanks. O.C. Coys will use the Hot Food Containers to carry them to their Areas.

No 11. **RECEIPTS.** All Trench Receipts must be sent to Orderly Room by 10 a.m. 26/5/16.

Issued at 9.0 a.m. 24/5/16.
Copy No 1 Filed.
2 War Diary.
3 "A" Coy.
4 "B" "
5 "C" "
6 "D" "
7 T.O.
8 Q.M.

(sgd) R.C.WILSON. Lieut.
Actg. Adjt. 15th Bn R.W.F.

BILLETS. 2nd Lieut B.Thomas "A" Coy will hand over billets, and will obtain a certificate as to their cleanliness. Before leaving O.C.Coys will inspect Billets and report to O.Room that they are clean.

OPERATION ORDER NO 17 BY LIEUT COLONEL R.C.BELL COMMDG 15th BN. R.W.F.

COPY NO 2 MAP REF. SHEET 36 and AREA "J" FOR 29.5.16.

RELIEF. The 15th Battalion R.W.F. will be relieved by the 16th R.W.F at 8.0 p.m. tomorrow May 29th.
"C" "D" and "B" Coys of the 15th R.W.F. will be relieved by "A" "B" and "C" Coys respectively of the 16th R.W.F.

PLATOON GUIDES. Platoon Guides from each of the above three Coys of the 15th R.W.F. will meet the relieving Coys of the 16th R.W.F. at ROUGE CROIX Cross Roads at 8.0 p.m.

The relief will be brought up as follows :-

"A" Coy 16th R.W.F. via SIGN POST LANE.
"B" Coy do via S. TILLELOY C.T.
"C" Coy do via ditto.

On relief, "C" "D" and "B" Coys of the 15th R.W.F. will proceed via S.TILLELOY C.T. and RUGBY ROAD to former Billets in REIZ BAILLEUL

POSTS. O.C. "A" Coy 15th R.W.F. will arrange relief of Posts with O.C. "D" Coy 16th R.W.F., the relief to be completed before 8.0 p.m.

LEWIS GUNS. M.G.O. will arrange relief of Lewis Guns in Posts.

TRANSPORT. Three Limbers will be at LA BASSEE CROSSING at 8.0 p.m. to receive all Battn. H.Q. M.O. and Coy H.Q. stuff.

BILLETS. Captain G.Owen D.S.O. will take over Billets at REIZ BAILL EUL in the afternoon.

RECEIPTS. All trench receipts, and Tactical Progress Reports up to time of relief to be handed into Orderly Room by 8.0 a.m. 30th inst.

(sgd) L.W.GRIFFITH.
Captain & Actg. Adjutant.
15th Battalion R.W.F.

Issued at 9.30 p.m. 28/5/16.
Copy No 1 Filed.
2 War Diary.
3 "A" Coy.
4 "B" "
5 "C" "
6 "D" "
7 Q.M. and T.O.
8 16th Bn R.W.F.

15 R.W. Fus

Army Form C. 2118

vol 6

June

Instructions regarding War Diaries and Intelligence Summaries are contained in F. S. Regs., Part II. and the Staff Manual respectively. Title Pages will be prepared in manuscript.

WAR DIARY
or
INTELLIGENCE SUMMARY

(Erase heading not required.)

Place	Date	Hour	Summary of Events and Information	Remarks and references to Appendices
			CONFIDENTIAL. WAR DIARY. OF 15th BATTALION. R.W.F. From 1st June 1916. To 30th June 1916 VOLUME VII.	49

1875 Wt. W593/826 1,000,000 4/15 J.B.C. & A. A.D.S.S./Forms/C. 2118.

Instructions regarding War Diaries and Intelligence Summaries are contained in F. S. Regs., Part II. and the Staff Manual respectively. Title Pages will be prepared in manuscript.

WAR DIARY
or
INTELLIGENCE SUMMARY
(Erase heading not required.)

Army Form C. 2118

Place	Date	Hour	Summary of Events and Information	Remarks and references to Appendices
RIEZ BAILLEUL	1 June		Battalion in support at RIEZ BAILLEUL	
	2	8 pm	Relieved 16th R.W.F in Moated Grange Section of trenches	
	3		In trenches: 2 O.R killed; Headquarters & 'C' Coy 1/2 Bucks (T.F) attached for instruction.	
	4	"	" " 3 " " wounded	
	5	"	" " no casualties	
	6	"	" " " 'D' Coy 1/2 Bucks (T.F) attached for instruction in place of 'C' Coy	
	7	"	" " 1 OR wounded	
	8	10 pm	Relieved by 16 RWF, & returned to RIEZ BAILLEUL in support. 2/5 Gloucesters (T.F) attached for instruction.	
	9	"	At RIEZ BAILLEUL	
	10	"	38th Division hands over Divisional Front to 61st Division (TF): Battalion relieved at Riez Bailleul 2/5 Worcesters. Division leaves XIth Corps.	
MERVILLE	11	"	Battalion moves to Merville	
BUSNETTES	12	"	" " " BUSNETTES	
	"	13	~~FLORINGHEM~~ Battalion rests at Busnettes	
FLORINGHEM	14		Battalion moves to FLORINGHEM. Daylight Saving adopted by B.E.F time put forward one hour at 11 pm.	
BAILLEUL-AUX CORNAILLES.	15		" " " BAILLEUL-AUX-CORNAILLES. 38th Div: joins 17th Corps	
	16		Divisional Training Commences	
	17		" "	
	18		" "	
	19		" "	
	20		" "	
	21		" "	
	22		" "	

R. C. Bell Lt. Col.
Comdg. 15th Bn. R.W.F.

6092

1875 Wt. W593/826 1,000,000 4/15 J.B.C. & A. A.D.S.S./Forms/C. 2118.

Army Form C. 2118

WAR DIARY
or
INTELLIGENCE SUMMARY
(Erase heading not required.)

Instructions regarding War Diaries and Intelligence Summaries are contained in F. S. Regs., Part II. and the Staff Manual respectively. Title Pages will be prepared in manuscript.

Place	Date	Hour	Summary of Events and Information	Remarks and references to Appendices
BAILLEUL-AUX CORNAILLES	23		Divisional Training	
	24		" "	
	25		" " ends.	
VACQUERIE-LE-BOUCQ.	26	5 pm	Battalion moves to VACQUERIE-LE-BOUCQ. 38th Div: joins IInd Corps.	
"	27	9 am	" " " BERNAVILLE.	
"	28	"	" rests at Bernaville.	
"	29	"	" " " "	
"	30	"	" " moves to PUCHEVILLERS.	

R. C. Bell. Lt-Col.
Comdg. 15th Bn. R.W.F.

1875 Wt. W593/826 1,000,000 4/15 J.B.C. & A. A.D.S.S./Forms/C. 2118.

113th Inf.Bde.
38th Div.

WAR DIARY

15th BATTN. THE ROYAL WELCH FUSILIERS.

J U L Y

1 9 1 6

Instructions regarding War Diaries and Intelligence Summaries are contained in F. S. Regs., Part II. and the Staff Manual respectively. Title Pages will be prepared in manuscript.

WAR DIARY
or
INTELLIGENCE SUMMARY
(Erase heading not required.)

Place	Date	Hour	Summary of Events and Information	Remarks and references to Appendices
			CONFIDENTIAL	
			WAR DIARY	
			of	
			15th BATTN. R.W.F.	
			(1st LONDON WELSH)	
			FROM 1st July 1916. TO 31st July 1916.	
			(Volume VII)	

1875 Wt. W593/826 1,000,000 4/15 J.B.C. & A. A.D.S.S./Forms/C. 2118.

Instructions regarding War Diaries and Intelligence Summaries are contained in F. S. Regs., Part II. and the Staff Manual respectively. Title Pages will be prepared in manuscript.

INTELLIGENCE SUMMARY

(Erase heading not required.)

Place	Date	Hour	Summary of Events and Information	Remarks and references to Appendices
PUCHEVILLERS	1st July.	–	Arrived Puchevillers midnight 31st June.	
"	2nd "	9 pm	Battalion moved to LEALVILLERS.	
LEALVILLERS	3	–	" at Lealvillers.	
"	3.	7 pm.	" moved to RIBEMONT, arriving 2. am 4th July.	
RIBEMONT.	4		" at Ribemont.	
MAMETZ.	5	12 Noon.	" moved to MAMETZ: occupied advanced trenches of 7th Division and relieved 1st WARWICKS in QUEEN'S NULLAH, BOTTOM WOOD, BUNNY ALLEY + BUNNY TRENCH, WHITE + CLIFF TRENCHES at 8.0 pm.	
	6.		Above trenches systematically bombarded by an Enemy Battery of 5.9" Howitzers on 5, 6 + 7th July: our Casualties: Capt. W.A. Howells – OC A Coy wounded, shellshock	
	7		5th July, Lt. I.H. Hughes, wounded 6 July. Lt. F.W.S. Harris wounded 7 July.	
	7	6.30 pm	Small operation ~~[illegible]~~ organised under Lt. R.V. Jones, OC A Coy against southern portion of MAMETZ Wood: Operation was not pushed as Enemy suddenly revealed his strength in Machine Guns, which covered approaches to the wood. In this operation Lt. F.W.S. Harris was wounded and 11 O.R. Killed + wounded.	
	7.8	2.30 am.	Relieved by 16 RWF and went into Brigade Reserve at MINDEN POST. Our Casualties from July 5 to 7th were:– 3 Officers wounded, 67 O.R. Killed and wounded.	
MINDEN POST.	8		Resting in Brigade Reserve.	
	9	12. noon.	Battalion moved through MAMETZ village into FRITZ and DANTZIG Trenches preparatory to a General attack by 38th (Welsh Division) on MAMETZ WOOD.	

1875 Wt. W593/826 1,000,000 4/15 J.B.C. & A. A.D.S.S./Forms/C. 2118.

Instructions regarding War Diaries and Intelligence Summaries are contained in F. S. Regs., Part II. and the Staff Manual respectively. Title Pages will be prepared in manuscript.

INTELLIGENCE SUMMARY

(Erase heading not required.)

Place	Date	Hour	Summary of Events and Information	Remarks and references to Appendices
MINDEN Post.	9	2.30 p.m.	Order received that operation was cancelled & Battalion moved back into Minden Post, arriving back by 6.30 p.m.	
		11.55 p.m.	Operation Order received for 38th (Welsh) Division to attack Mametz Wood at 3.15 am.	
	10		10 July '16, 113th Infantry Bde. on left of 114 Inf. Bde.: 15th Batt. RWF in Reserve to 14th & 16th RWF under G.O.C. Bde.	
MAMETZ WOOD	10.	2.15 am.	Battalion in position in BUNNY TRENCH.	
		4.15 am.	moved and was in attack formation between QUEEN'S NULLAH and WHITE TRENCH, formed into four lines in Coys. A Coy. leading. behind 14 RWF. B.C & D Coys following. ~~Vide appendix for details of this operation.~~ 22	~~Vide~~ 22
	10-11		Casualties in this action. Lt. R.G. Rees. Killed. 2/Lt. R.A. Fleming missing. Lt. R.C. Wilson. wounded. Lt. A.T.M. Williams " (died of wounds 19/7/16.) 2/Lt. C. Ellis " 2/Lt. J.S. Leach " 2/Lt. B. Thomas " Lt Col. R.C. Bell. " (at duty) Capt. H.B. Day. Rame. " Casualties. O.R. 20 Killed. 132 wounded 19 missing (2 since traced Killed, 2 " " died of wounds, 8 " " wounded)	

1875 Wt. W593/826 1,000,000 4/15 J.B.C. & A. A.D.S.S./Forms/C. 2118.

Instructions regarding War Diaries and Intelligence Summaries are contained in F. S. Regs., Part II. and the Staff Manual respectively. Title Pages will be prepared in manuscript.

INTELLIGENCE SUMMARY

(Erase heading not required.)

Place	Date	Hour	Summary of Events and Information	Remarks and references to Appendices
MAMETZ WOOD.	July 10-11		Officers who proceeded into action. Lt. Col. R.C. Bell. (Commanding) Major. J. Edwards (2nd in C.). Capt. T. Elias (Adjutant). Capt. E.M. Burrell (signals) 2 Lt. S.G. Fitzsimons (Lewis Guns) A Coy. Lt. R.C. Wilson (O.C.) wounded. 2/Lt. W.J. Ellis. 2/Lt. H.J. Cundall. B Coy. Capt. L.N.V. Evans (O.C.) Lt. R.G. Rees. (Killed) Lt. E. Davies. C Coy. Lt. H.T.M. Williams (O.C.) wounded. 2/Lt. B. Thomas. wounded. 2/Lt. T.E. Leach (11 Glosters attd.) wounded. D Coy. Lt. H.V. Williams (O.C.) 2nd Lt. C. Ellis. wounded. 2nd Lt. R.H. Fleming. Missing. M.O. Capt. H.B. Day. ~~R~~ RAMC Prisoners. The Battalion captured between 80-90 of prisoners taken by the Division. Other Captures. The battalion captured 4 Enemy Machine Guns.	
"	11	10am.	Relieved in Wood by 16 RWF and withdrew to QUEENS NULLAH.	Relief complete 1.15 pm.
		2 pm.	Relieved by 115th Inf. Bde.	
RIBEMONT.		6.30pm.	Battalion marched to RIBEMONT.	
ERGNIES.	12.	9am.	Battalion ~~[illegible]~~ entrained at MERICOURT for LONGPRE: marched from LONGPRE to ERGNIES.	
	13		Battalion resting at Ergnies.	

1875 Wt. W593/826 1,000,000 4/15 J.B.C. & A. A.D.S.S./Forms/C. 2118.

Instructions regarding War Diaries and Intelligence Summaries are contained in F. S. Regs., Part II. and the Staff Manual respectively. Title Pages will be prepared in manuscript.

INTELLIGENCE SUMMARY

(Erase heading not required.)

Place	Date	Hour	Summary of Events and Information	Remarks and references to Appendices
ERGNIES	July 14		Battn. resting at ERGNIES.	
AUTHIE	15	10 a.m.	Battn. proceeds in Motor Buses to AUTHIE.	
	16		" resting at AUTHIE.	
	17	11.30 a.m.	Battn. inspected and welcomed into VIII th Corps by Major Genl. Sir Aylmer Hunter Weston.	
COUIN.	"	3.30 p.m.	" moved into bivouacs near COUIN.	
COIGNEUX	18	2. p.m.	" moved to bivouacs near COIGNEUX.	
"	19		RSM. J.R. Jones awarded Military Cross by G.O.C. in C.	
	18-24		Battn. in COIGNEUX, supplies working parties for 114 & 115 th Inf. Bdes. in HEBUTERNE ~~Sector~~. trench Sector.	
	24	2.15 p.m.	Battn. relieved 8th Royal Fusiliers (12th Division) in AUCHONVILLERS Left Sub-Section. front line.	
AUCHONVILLERS.	24-28		In above trenches: no incidents of note: Casualties - 3 O.R. wounded.	
"	28	11.30 A.M.	Battn. relieved by 12th Kings Liverpool Regt. (20th Division).	
BUS-LES-ARTOIS	28	"	Battn. marched to BUS-LES-ARTOIS.	
THIEVRES	29	7 a.m.	Battn. marched to THIEVRES.	
	30	"	" in Thievres.	
	30/31	12.19	" marched to DOULLENS and entrained for HOPOUTRE near POPERINGHE, arriving 6.30 a.m.	

1875 Wt. W593/826 1,000,000 4/15 J.B.C. & A. A.D.S.S./Forms/C. 2118.

and the Staff Manual respectively. Title Pages will be prepared in manuscript.

(Erase heading not required.)

Place	Date	Hour	Summary of Events and Information	Remarks and references to Appendices
Herzeele.	July 31.	7 am.	Battalion marched to HERZEELE, arriving 2.30 p.m.	

R. C. Bell. Lt. Col.
Comdg. 15th Batt (1st London Welsh) Royal Welsh Fusiliers.
1. 8. 16.

1875 Wt. W593/826 1,000,000 4/15 J.B.C. & A. A.D.S.S./Forms/C. 2118.

Vol 8

15. BATT. R.W.F

WAR DIARY FOR AUGUST 1916

WAR DIARY
or
INTELLIGENCE SUMMARY
(Erase heading not required.)

Instructions regarding War Diaries and Intelligence Summaries are contained in F. S. Regs., Part II. and the Staff Manual respectively. Title Pages will be prepared in manuscript.

Army Form C. 2118

a 147

Place	Date	Hour	Summary of Events and Information	Remarks and references to Appendices

CONFIDENTIAL

WAR DIARY

— of —

15th BATTN. R. W. F.
(London Welsh)

From 1st August 1916

To. August 31st 1916

Volume VIII

1875 Wt. W593/826 1,000,000 4/15 J.B.C. & A. A.D.S.S./Forms/C. 2118.

Instructions regarding War Diaries and Intelligence Summaries are contained in F. S. Regs., Part II. and the Staff Manual respectively. Title Pages will be prepared in manuscript.

WAR DIARY
or
~~INTELLIGENCE SUMMARY~~
(Erase heading not required.)

Army Form C. 2118

Place	Date	Hour	Summary of Events and Information	Remarks and references to Appendices
HERZEELE	1/8/16		Battalion resting after entrainment from DOULLENS to HOPOUTRE near POPERINGHE and march thence to HERZEELE.	
ST. JAN TER BIEZEN.	2/8/16.		Battalion moved into camp "L" S.W. of ST JAN TER BIEZEN taking over camp from 9th NORFOLKS	
	3-20/8/16		Training.	
YPRES.	20/8/16	10pm-2am	Battalion entrained at POPERINGHE to ASYLUM. YPRES. Relieved 1st Royal Irish Fusiliers	
	21/8/16		in Support along West of CANAL BANK, S.W. of PILCKEM. and S.E. of BOESINGHE (Left. sub-section	
	22/8/16		ST JULIEN)	
	23/8/16.		"A" and "B" Coys moved into Front Line, relieving two Companies of 2nd Battalion SEAFORTH HIGHLANDERS.	
	21-22/8/16	midnight	Enemy Patrol, 25 strong, attempting to surprise a small post held by 'A' Company dispersed by Rifle and Lewis Gun fire.	
	24/8/16 25/8/16		Relieved 16th R.W.F. in Front Line.	
	26/8/16 27/8/16		Casualties – 1. O.R. Killed. 2. O.R. Wounded.	
	28/8/16 29/8/16 30/8/16 31/8/16.		In support along W. of Canal Bank.	

R. C. Bell. Lt Col
Comdg. 15th Bn. R.W.F.
1.9.16.

1875 Wt. W593/826 1,000,000 4/15 J.B.C. & A. A.D.S.S./Forms/C. 2118.

– WAR DIARY –

15th BATTALION R.W.F.

FOR

SEPTEMBER 1916.

Vol 9

9 D
2 sheets

Instructions regarding War Diaries and Intelligence Summaries are contained in F. S. Regs., Part II. and the Staff Manual respectively. Title Pages will be prepared in manuscript.

WAR DIARY
or
~~INTELLIGENCE SUMMARY~~
(Erase heading not required.)

Army Form C. 2118

Place	Date	Hour	Summary of Events and Information	Remarks and references to Appendices
	Sept.			
YPRES	1		Relieved 16 RIoF in Front Line. Left sub-section. (Left Sector) ST. JULIEN (Casualty 1)	
	2-3		in Front Line	
	4		do (Casualty 1)	
	5		do Corps Commander, Lt. Gen Hunter-Weston visited trenches	
	6.		do (Casualty 1)	
	7		do. Were relieved by 10th SWB's and returned to Divisional Reserve at 'E' Camp.	
	8		In 'E' Camp. Men on Nightly working parties, alternately on line & in surrounding Camps.	
	9-12		do do do	
	13		do 2/Lt. W.T. Ellis wounded in Bombing accident while training Raiding Party. 2 O.R. wounded. & 2 O.R. wounded	at duty.
	14-16		do.	
	17		Relieved 10th SWB's in Left Support. CANAL BANK	
	18.		In Left Support. CANAL BANK	
	19		do do. Lt. Col. R.C. Bell rejoined his Unit. (Central Indian Horse) Major C.C. Norman took over Command.	
	20-21		Left Support. CANAL BANK	
	22		Relieved 16th RWF in Front Line. Left sub-section. ST. JULIEN	
	23-25		Front Line.	
	26.		Post E29 bombed by Germans. – Casualties. 1 O.R. Killed. 4 O.R. Wounded. 3 O.R. wounded accidly.	
	27.		Relieved by 16th RWF. Retd. to Left Support CANAL BANK. Casualties 1 O.R. Wounded 2 O.R. Wounded	at duty. (1 S. Shock)
	28-30.		LEFT SUPPORT. CANAL BANK.	

C.C. Norman Lt. Col.
Comg 18th R.W.F.

1875 Wt. W593/826 1,000,000 4/15 J.B.C. & A. A.D.S.S./Forms/C. 2118.

Vol 10

WAR DIARY.

OF

15TH BATTALION.

ROYAL WELSH FUSILIERS.

OCTOBER 1916

Instructions regarding War Diaries and Intelligence Summaries are contained in F. S. Regs., Part II. and the Staff Manual respectively. Title Pages will be prepared in manuscript.

WAR DIARY
or
INTELLIGENCE SUMMARY
(Erase heading not required.)

Army Form C. 2118

Place	Date	Hour	Summary of Events and Information	Remarks and references to Appendices
			CONFIDENTIAL WAR DIARY — of — 15th Batt R. W. F. (LONDON WELSH) From October 1st 1916. To October 31st 1916. Volume X C. C. Norman Lt Col Comd 15th R.W.F.	

1875 Wt. W593/826 1,000,000 4/15 J.B.C. & A. A.D.S.S./Forms/C. 2118.

Instructions regarding War Diaries and Intelligence Summaries are contained in F. S. Regs., Part II. and the Staff Manual respectively. Title Pages will be prepared in manuscript.

WAR DIARY
or
INTELLIGENCE SUMMARY
(Erase heading not required.)

Army Form C. 2118

Place	Date	Hour	Summary of Events and Information	Remarks and references to Appendices
Elverdinghe. Sector. Ypres.	1st Oct.		Battalion holding front line trenches, being the extreme left Battalion of the B. E. F. and joining up with the French on the YPRES CANAL Sth of BOESINGHE	
	2nd		In front line 1 O. R. Killed	
	3rd		" " " Lieut G. H. Porter. killed (buried about one mile N of Ypres. between the Canal and Boesinghe	
	4th		" " " 2nd Lt W. Warwick Jones (wounded concussion). 2 O.R. Killed 1. O.R. Wounded.	
	5th		" " " One O.R. Killed Relieved by 16th R.W.F. 7.35.p.m	
	6th		In Support along West of Ypres Canal Bank.	
	7		" "	
	8		" "	
	9		Relieved 16th R.W.F. in Front Line 7.30.p.m.	
	10		In Front Line	
	11		" " "	
	12.		" " 5 O.R. Wounded in advanced post called E29	
	13.		" " At 8.p.m. a special party under four Officers raided German trenches securing four prisoners, Casualties 13. O.R. Wounded. 1 OR Missing	Scheme & Narrative attached
	14.		" " At 9.30. p.m. relieved by 10th S.W.B. 115th Infantry Brigade after relief Battalion returned to Camp E, to Divisional Reserve.	

1875 Wt. W593/826 1,000,000 4/15 J.B.C. & A. A.D.S.S./Forms/C. 2118.

Army Form C. 2118

WAR DIARY
or
INTELLIGENCE SUMMARY

(Erase heading not required.)

Instructions regarding War Diaries and Intelligence Summaries are contained in F. S. Regs., Part II. and the Staff Manual respectively. Title Pages will be prepared in manuscript.

Place	Date	Hour	Summary of Events and Information	Remarks and references to Appendices
ELVERDINGHE Sector. Ypres.	15th		In Camp E. Resting	
	16.		" " . . . . Training & Working	
	17.		. . . . . Inspection by 2nd Army Commander. Gen. Sir Herbert C. O. Plumer. who presented MILITARY MEDALS. to the following for gallantry during raid on night of Oct: 13th.	
			No 22158. Pte. A. Briggs.	
			No 27213. Pte. A.E. Ford	
			No 22539. Pte. A.E. Lewis.	
	18th		" "	
	19.		" "	
	20.		" "	
	21st		" "	
	22nd		" "	
	23rd		" " Inspected by VIII Corps Commander Lt. Gen Sir AYLMER, HUNTER, WESTON who presented MILITARY CROSS. to following Officers. for their determination, bravery and devotion to duty during raid Oct. 13th.	
			2nd Lt W. M. MORGAN (previously awarded Albert Medal. class II)	
			2nd Lt. Ray. Bowes.	
			Another Officer 2nd Lt. R. T. WILSON-JONES. also awarded MILITARY CROSS but was not decorated, being in hospital.	
	24th	8.p.m.	Relieved 10th S.W.B's in Reserve. on CANAL BANK.	
	25	"	11th S.W.B's in Front Line	
	26		In Front Line 1. O.R. Killed 1 O.R. Wounded	
	27			

1875 Wt. W593/826 1,000,000 4/15 J.B.C. & A. A.D.S.S./Forms/C. 2118.

Instructions regarding War Diaries and Intelligence Summaries are contained in F. S. Regs., Part II. and the Staff Manual respectively. Title Pages will be prepared in manuscript.

WAR DIARY
or
INTELLIGENCE SUMMARY
(Erase heading not required.)

Army Form C. 2118

Place	Date	Hour	Summary of Events and Information	Remarks and references to Appendices
ELVERDINGHE Sector. Ypres.	28.		In front Line 1 O. R. Wounded.	
	29		" " "	
	30		" " " 2nd Lt. J. G. EVANS. wounded. Three Companys relieved by 16th R.W.F.	
	31st		Battalion in Support. W. CANAL BANK. (less A. Coy which came into support. (6.30.p.m. 1 O.R. Killed 1 O.R. Wounded.	
			NOTE. Honours awarded to Battalion which were omitted in September Diary Military Medals No 22354. Pte. L. S. Rogers. 22998. Pte. R. J. Shoulder. (attached & subsequently transferred to 113th M.G.C.) 8999. Sergt. G. W. Jones. (from 2nd Batt R.W.F. 11192. Pte. C. Lloyd. " " " "	

C. C. Norman Lt Col
Comd 15th R.W.F.

1875 Wt. W593/826 1,000,000 4/15 J.B.C. & A. A.D.S.S./Forms/C. 2118.

RAID.

~~TO BE~~ CARRIED OUT BY 15th BATTALION R.W.F.
ON NIGHT 12/13th OCT. 1916.

1. OBJECT OF RAID. To enter the German Trenches at G 13 b [illegible].8 To kill Germans or take prisoners, and so to obtain identifications.

2. INFORMATION. The German trench is a double one, consisting of a fire trench with a parrallell supervision trench 10 to 15 yards in rear connected at intervals of about 40 yards by short communication trenches. Such trenches are usually manned by double sentries at intervals along the fire trench, the remainder of the sentry groups being kept in the supervision trench. Working parties moving trolleys are frequently heard at night in rear of the trench. These would probably take refuge from the bombardment in the supervision trench. They commence work only after dark, and generally at a late hour in the evening.

3. STRENGTH AND DISTRIBUTION OF PARTIES.

	Off.	N.C.O's	Men.
Reconnoitring Patrol.	1		2
SUPPORT TRENCH PARTY.			
Right Blocking Party.		1	4
Left Blocking Party.	1	1	4
Clearing Party.		1	4
FIRE TRENCH PARTY.			
Right Blocking Party.		1	4
Left Blocking Party.	1	1	4
Clearing Party.		1	4
COVERING PARTIES.			
Right Covering Party.		1	8
Left Covering Party.		1	8
	1		
REAR PARTY.			
Escort to Prisoners.		1	6
Stretcher Bearers.		-	4
Total.	4	9	52

4. EQUIPMENT.

OFFICERS. Revolvers. Knobkerry. Whistle.

BLOCKING PARTIES. N.C.O's. Revolvers. Wire cutters Knobkerries. Whistles.

BOMBERS. (2) 24 bombs in Bomb bag. Knobkerries.

RIFLE MEN. Rifle and Bayonet. Wirecutters and clasp knives.

CLEARING PARTIES. N.C.O's Revolvers. Torch. Whistle.

BOMBERS. (2) 12 Bombs in Bomb Bag Knobkerries. 2 Smoke Bombs.

BAYONET MEN. (2) Rifle and Bayonet. Wirecutters.

RECONNOITRING PATROL. COVERING PARTY AND ESCORT TO PRISONERS. N.C.O's and men. Rifles and Bayonets.

SPECIAL EQUIPMENT.
Three mats for crossing enemy's wire.
Roll of 300 yards of telephone wire and three discs painted black on one side and with luminous paint on the opposite side. (For the Reconnoitring Patrol)
White linen for distinguishing marks for the columns.

5. PLAN. 1. It is proposed to cut a gap in the enemy's wire opposite the point of entry by artillery fire during the afternoon of the day of the Raid.

2. To move the party out into "NO MAN'S LAND" in front of our own wire after dark, and to send a patrol to mark the gap by laying a wire and placing discs to indicate the position of the gap.

3. Then to bombard the objective heavily with trench mortars and Guns with the object of reducing the enemy's moral and breaking up his parapet.

4. To move forward the Raiding Party ~~through-the-gap-and into-the-enemy's-fire-and-support-trenches-under-cover-of an-artille-y-barrage.~~ at the moment when the Trench Mortar fire ceases under cover of an artillery barrage.

5. To rush the Raiding Party through the gap and into the enemy's fire and support trenches under cover of an artillery barrage.

6. To withdraw after 10 minutes in the enemy trenches.

6. OPERATIONS. - 2 hours. Reconnoitring patrol moves out.

- 30 minutes. Raiding Party leaves our parapet and moves to position in front of our wire.

Zero. Trench Mortar bombardment of objective commences.
Howitzer Fire on C 13 b 6¼.8. C 14 a 3¼.3 and C 14 a 4.2
Raiders crawl forward.

14 Intense artillery bombardment of objective.

16 Trench Mortar bombardment shifts from objective to flanks.

17 Artillery bombardment shifts from objective to barrage. Raiding Party enters enemy trenches.

27 Raiding Party commences to withdraw.

Artillery barrage ceases when O.C. Raid gives instructions, probably about 37

O.C. 113th Machine Gun Company will arrange for direct or overhead fire in "NO MAN'S LAND" and SOUTH of the line of advance, commencing at Zero and ceasing when artillery ceases. The O.C. 15th Battn R.W.F. will arrange for Lewis Gun Fire.

7. ASSEMBLY. Parties will form up on the CANAL BANK in the following order from front to rear preparatory to moving up the communication trenches.

ASSEMBLY. (Contd)

SUPERVISION TRENCH PARTY.	(Officer. (N.C.O. (Riflemen. (Bombers.	) Right Blocking Party.
	(N.C.O. (Riflemen. (Bombers.	) Left Blocking Party.
	(N.C.O. (Men.	) Clearing Party.
	(Officer. (N.C.O. (Riflemen. (Bombers.	) Right Blocking Party.
FIRE TRENCH.	(N.C.O. (Riflemen. (Bombers.	) Left Blocking Party.
	(N.C.O. (Men.	) Clearing Party.
FLANKING PARTIES.	(Officer. (N.C.O. (Men	) Right Flanking Party.
	(N.C.O. (Men.	) Left Flanking Party.
REAR PARTY.	(N.C.O. (Men.	) Escort to Prisoners.

8. **ADVANCE.**

The Raiding Party will cross our own Parapet at three points which will be marked CENTRE - RIGHT - LEFT - by means of steps prepared during the day. They will pass through a gap in our own wire to be cut on the night preceding the Raid, and they will move across "NO MAN'S LAND" in three columns.

LEFT COLUMN. (FIRE TRENCH PARTY.)	CENTRE COLUMN. (SUPPT TRENCH PARTY)	RIGHT COLUMN. (FIRE TRENCH) PARTY)
Left Blocking Party.	Officer. Right Blocking Party. Left Blocking Party.	Right Blocking Party.
(Covering Party.) Left Flankers.	Clearing Party. (Fire Trench Party) Officer. Clearing Party. (Rear Party) Officer. Escort to Prisoners.	(Covering Party) Right Flankers.

DISTINGUISHING MARKS will be :-

CENTRE COLUMN. - White Patch on back.
RIGHT COLUMN. - White band on right arm.
LEFT COLUMN. - White band on left arm.

9. **DUTIES OF PARTIES.**

SUPPORT TRENCH PARTY. will cross the Fire trench and enter the Support Trench.
The Right Blocking Party will form a block at the point of entry.
The Left Blocking Party will move to the left and will form a block about 30 yards from the Right Blocking Pa[rty]
The Clearing Party will follow the Left Blocking Part[y]
and will bomb all dug-outs and secure prisoners.

identifications, and material.
FIRE TRENCH PARTY will enter the Fire Trench and act in the same manner as the Support Trench Party.
COVERING PARTY. The Right and Left Covering Parties will remain outside the wire to cover the flanks while the Support and Fire Trench Parties are in the trench, and to cover the withdrawal. They will each furnish a double sentry to watch the Flanks of the line of approach. These parties will move out to about 30 yards on the flank of the Raiders during the time the advance is being made from our wire.
REAR PARTY. Escort to Prisoners will remain outside the trench behind the parapet ready to remove prisoners, carry back identifications, and assist wounded.

10. THE WITHDRAWAL. Parties will withdraw after 10 minutes in the trenches in the following order :-

ESCORT TO PRISONERS.	-	FIRST.
SUPPORT TRENCH PARTY.	-	SECOND.
FIRE TRENCH PARTY.	-	THIRD.
COVERING PARTIES.	-	LAST.

The signal for the withdrawal will be long and short blasts on the whistle, alternately.

11. TIMING. Watches of Raiders will be synchronized at Left Group Headquarters before starting.
A Raiding Officer will synchronize watches of T.M. Officers at BUTT 17 at Zero - 1 Hour.
The D.T.M.O. will arrange for the T.M.Officers to be there.

12. COMMUNICATIONS O.C. Raiding Party with 6 runners will maintain communication with Battalion Headquarters from point of exit from our own parapet.
He will report :-
1. Time of departure of Raiding Party from our parapet.
2. Time Raiders enter German Trench.
3. Send down identifications as they come in.
4. Time withdrawal commences.
5. Raiders all in.
6. Results of Raid.

1. 2. 4. 5. by CODE on telephone from point of exit.

3. By Runner to Battalion Headquarters.

6. Shortly by telephone. He will then proceed to Brigade H.Qtrs with the Raiding Officers to make a full Report.

26/10/16.

(sgd) C.C.H. NORMAN.
Lieut. Colonel.
Commanding 15th Battalion R. W. F.

15 RWF Oct 1916

10

38th Division No.G.S.498.

V111 Corps.

REPORT ON RAID CARRIED OUT BY15TH R.W.F. ON NIGHT 13/14TH OCTOBER 1916 ON GERMAN LINE AT C.13.b.9.8.

Leader Lt H.V. Williams

Under cover of a heavy Stokes Mortar and Artillery bombardment the raiding party of 4 Officers 61 Other ranks of 15th R.W.F. drew up in NO MAN'S LAND.

Two hostile machine guns, and one on each flank gave some trouble as the party went out but they appeared to be silenced by our Artillery, as afterwards they did not fireagain.

The bombardment lifted at 8.18.p.m. and the raiders rushed the trench. The wire had been well cut by the Artillery, and only one party had occasion to use mats. One party on entering the front line went to the left and about 15 yards from the point of entry, found a dug-out containing four Germans who were made prisoners. Another party proceeded along a short communication trench to the supervision trench about 20 yards in rear of the front line.

Practically no opposition was met with, the Stokes Mortar bombardment having done considerable damage to the German trenches

A few bombs were thrown at the party as they went through the enemy wire, and again as they withdrew; these latter seemed to come from behind the Supervision trench. Party withdrew at 8.30.p.m, bringing with them the four prisoners one of whom is an Unter Offizier, all belonging to the 1st Battalion, 1st Guards Reserve Regt. A certain amount of equipment was also brought away.

~~XXXXXXXXXXXXXX~~.

Enemy retaliation for our bombardment was feeble and ill-directed; most of it seemed to fall about 20 yards behind our front line; a certaim amount about LANCASHIRE FARM. The Stokes Mortars fired 1500 rounds.

ENEMY CASUALTIES.

4 or 5 killed, a few wounded seen in the trench.

4 prisoners.

OUR CASUALTIES.

9 other ranks wounded (mostly slight.)

REPORT ON RAID CARRIED OUT BY 13TH WELSH REGT ON NIGHT 13/14TH OCTOBER 1916 AT C.22.a.2.7.

A raiding party of 2 Officers 52 other ranks of 13th Welsh Regt, left our trenches at 7.35.p.m. and moved into position in NO MAN'S LAND with the object of entering the German trenches at C.22.a.2.7.

The wire at this point had been previously cut by Artillery and Trench Mortars.

Unfortunately, owing to the brightness of the moon the party was seen from Sap 10, and numerous Very lights were sent up. At the same time a heavy M.G. and Trench Mortar fire was opened on the raiding party, accompanied by considerable fire from hostile artillery, causing a number of casualties.

The fire increased causing some confusion amongst the raiders, with the result that some of the partiesgot mixed up, making it impossible to get through the hostile wire. The party accordingly withdrew about 8.15.p.m.

CASUALTIES.

2 other ranks killed (bodies recovered)

8 other ranks wounded.

Arthur J. Smith Capt
for Major General

14-10-16. Commanding 38th(Welsh) Division.

NARRATIVE OF RAID CARRIED OUT BY 15th BATTALION ROYAL WELSH FUSILIERS ON THE NIGHT OF 13/14th OCTOBER 1916.

ZERO WAS FIXED FOR 8.0 p.m.

1.

PRELIMINARY RECONNAISSANCE.

From Friday October 6th until the day of the Raid, reconnaissances of the ground up to the point at which the wire was to be cut by the artillery was carried out by 2/Lieut W.M.MORGAN and two men every evening. During this period it was ascertained that the going in "NO MAN'S LAND" was good, the exact direction in which the Raiders were to be led was noted, and pickets to mark the points at which luminous discs were to be put out on the night of the Raid were got into position.

During this period also all the Officers and N.C.O's of the Raiding Party were sent out over the parapet to familiarize them with the ground.

WIRE CUTTING.

The wire was cut by the artillery between 10.0 a.m. and 11.30 on the morning of the Raid. It was subsequently shown to have been so well cut that it offered no serious obstacle.

RECONNOITRING PATROL.

At 6.30 p.m. on the night of the Raid 2/Lieut MORGAN accompanied by the two men of his Patrol with four more men to give him additional protection, moved over our parapet and proceeded to put out the luminous discs. Three German Machine Guns were firing almost continuously across"NO MAN'S LAND". One from about C 14 c 4.2 firing North West;another from near C 14 a 1.7 firing towards E 28 and the third from the German Support Trench in rear and rather to the Left of the point of entry.

Owing to the delay caused by these Machine Guns it was not until nearly 8.0 p.m. that the last disc was in position, and 2/Lieut MORGAN had reconnoitred the gap and found it passable.

2/Lieut MORGAN then hurried back with the object of guiding the Raiders to the gap.

In the dark he missed them, but subsequently caught them up and entered the German Trench with them. The remainder of the Reconnoitring Patrol joined the Raiding Party just as they were moving forward.

THE CROSSING OF OUR PARAPET.

At 7.30 p.m. (the moment arranged for crossing the parapet) a German Machine Gun opened fire. The party waited until this ceased and then crossed and ~~them~~ moved on towards the three discs upon which the columns were to form up. As the columns were forming up about 30 or 40 rounds of Shrapnel were fired by the Germans at E 28 and in rear of E 27 and a heavy Machine Gun fire was directed almost continuously by them across "NO MAN'S LAND". This caused momentarily some slight confusion and the men, in some instances, went out of their places. Everyone was in his place by the time our own bombardment began. ~~They ad~~

THE ADVANCE TO THE WIRE.

At 8.0 p.m. when our bombardment commenced the whole party started to crawl forward under a heavy though ineffective Machine Gun fire. At about 8.4 or 8.5 p.m. the German Machine Gun fire ceased, probably silenced by our Trench Mortars and Guns. The Raiders, finding they were not being fired upon, stood up, and continued the advance, upright. The Raiders reached the gaps in the enemy's wire in good order at about 8.16 p.m. At this moment bombs, apparently thrown from somewhere behind the Supervision Trench, fell into the wire in front of, as well as to the right of, the right column.

Our own shrapnel was bursting over the trench and the leader of the Fire Trench Left Blocking Party was wounded by one of them. 2/Lieut WOOD at once took his place.

THE ASSAULT.

At about 8.16 or 8.17 p.m. (i.e. one or two minutes before the time arranged) the three columns almost simultaneously rushed through the wire in three different places. Only the Centre column found it necessary to use a mat, which was successfully thrown over the wire.

DESCRIPTION OF GERMAN TRENCH.

The Fire Trench, which had been revetted with good wooden hurdles, and was deep, had been almost obliterated by our own fire. It was scarcely recognisable towards the right and very badly damaged near the left of the Communication Trench.

The Supervision Trench had been so badly knocked in that it was very difficult to recognise.

The Communicating Trench was in good condition and was well revetted with stout timber. Dug-outs were found at the points indicated on the accompanying diagram.

SUPPORT TRENCH PARTY.

Bombs thrown into the wire wounded or knocked down the Officer and four men of the Support Trench Party. The remainder, however reached their appointed places. Clearing Party found one small dug-out, but this was so badly knocked about that it was impossible to enter. One prisoner was taken and one German was killed (by 2/Lieut MORGAN) in this trench.

FIRE TRENCH PARTY.

The Right Blocking Party reached the point allotted to them complete. Of the left Blocking Party the N.C.O. was wounded and one man knocked down, but the remainder carried on and reached their point. This party crossed through the wire at about 6 or more yards to the left of the Centre Column, with the result that the dugout (A) was missed by them at first. Subsequently three prisoners were taken. The trench was searched and Identifications collected.

ESCORT TO PRISONERS.

This party reached the point allotted to them, and when the prisoners and identifications were handed over to them, they brought them in.

COVERING PARTIES.

The Right Covering Party moved out to about 40 yards to the right when the columns moved forward from the starting point, and then, keeping parallel to the columns, moved up to the wire. The enemy were bombing their wire. Only one rifle shot was heard and Signal Lights were observed being sent up from the Support Trench in rear. A Machine Gun opened from a long way off on the right during the time the Raiders were in. The Left Covering Party moved out about 30 yards to the left and advanced in a parallel course to the columns up to the wire. Enemy were throwing bombs into the wire.

Both parties waited until all the Raiders had passed through and then retired.

THE WITHDRAWAL.

All parties withdrew in quick time. The escort and prisoners went first, 2/Lieut BOWES and the Support Trench Party next, then 2/Lieut WILSON JONES with the Fire Trench Party and finally the covering parties under 2/Lieut WOOD and 2/Lieut MORGAN. They were under an ineffective Machine Gun fire, from a point well away to the South, all the way across.

CASUALTIES.

GERMANS.

Killed by bombardment.	5
Killed by Raiders.	1
Total counted.	6
Prisoners.	5

one of whom was badly wounded and left behind in the German wire.

OUR CASUALTIES.

Killed.	none.
Wounded. (2 at duty)	12
Missing.	1
Total.	13

GENERAL.

During the whole period that the Raiding Party were in the Trench they were subjected to an almost continuous shower of Bombs, thrown apparently from somewhere in rear of the German Trench. It was these bombs which caused nearly all the casualties.

There is no definite information, as to any Germans, other than those already mentioned, having been seen.

In spite of all the bombs that were thrown and that the trench was almost knocked out of recognition it is remarkable that representatives of every Party reached the points allotted to them, but such undoubtedly was the case. Some Officers and some of the men spoke of confusion in the trench, but probably it is more apparent than real.

(sgd) C.C.NORMAN.
Lieut Colonel Commanding
15th Battalion R. W. F.

14/10/1916.

WAR DIARY

Vol XI

FOR

NOVEMBER 1916

15th BATTALION

ROYAL WELSH FUSILIERS

Instructions regarding War Diaries and Intelligence Summaries are contained in F. S. Regs., Part II. and the Staff Manual respectively. Title Pages will be prepared in manuscript.

WAR DIARY
or
INTELLIGENCE SUMMARY
(Erase heading not required.)

Army Form C. 2118

Place	Date	Hour	Summary of Events and Information	Remarks and references to Appendices
			CONFIDENTIAL WAR DIARY — of — 15a. BATT. R. W. F. (LONDON WELSH) From 1st November 1916. To. 30. November 1916 Volume. XI	

Norman Lt Col Comd 15 R W F

1875 Wt. W593/826 1,000,000 4/15 J.B.C. & A. A.D.S.S./Forms/C. 2118.

Army Form C. 2118.

Instructions regarding War Diaries and Intelligence Summaries are contained in F. S. Regs., Part II. and the Staff Manual respectively. Title pages will be prepared in manuscript.

WAR DIARY
or
INTELLIGENCE SUMMARY.

(Erase heading not required.)

Place	Date	Hour	Summary of Events and Information	Remarks and references to Appendices
YPRES. ELVERDINGHE SECTOR.	1.11.16.		In Support along West of YSER CANAL BANK. 2. OR. Wounded (1 at duty)	
	2.11.16		——— do ———	
	3.11.16		——— do ———	
	4.11.16.		Relieved 16th R.W.F. in Front Line. 4.30 pm.	
	5		In front Line.	
	6		"	
	7		"	
	8		"	
	9		Relieved in front line by 16 RWF. 8.0 pm. A. B. C. Coys returned to Canal Bank. D Coy to TROIS TOURS Chateau.	
	10		——— do ———	
	11		——— do ———	
	12.		——— do ———	
	13			
	14.		Relieved by 11th Battn S.W.B. relief complete 8.0 pm. Battalion moved in ~~Brigade~~ Divisional Reserve D Camp	

T2134. Wt. W708—776. 500000. 4/15. Sir J. C. & S.

Instructions regarding War Diaries and Intelligence Summaries are contained in F. S. Regs., Part II. and the Staff Manual respectively. Title pages will be prepared in manuscript.

WAR DIARY
or
INTELLIGENCE SUMMARY.

(Erase heading not required.)

Army Form C. 2118.

Place	Date	Hour	Summary of Events and Information	Remarks and references to Appendices
	15		Battalion in Reserve in D Camp, until 4.30 pm when it moved into E Camp	
	16		" " " - E Camp. Training & Resting	
	17		do	
	18		do	
	19.		Battn attached to 114th Inf Bde. and. do	
	20.		Relieved 13th Welsh Regt in Support on Left Canal Bank, Right Sub sector.	
	21		In Support Left Canal Bank.	
	22		do	
	23.		do.	
	24		do	
	25		Relieved by 13th Battn Welsh Regt, and on relief moved over to Right Canal Bank in Support.	
	26.		do	
	27		do	
	28		Relieved 16th Bn. R.W.F in front line. Relief complete 6.45 pm	
	29.		Battn in front line. 48 prisoners of 86 R.I.R. were taken at 6.0 am.	
	30		do	

T2134. Wt. W708-776. 500000, 4/15. Sir J. C. & S.

15th. BATTn. ROYAL WELSH FUSILIERS.

Vol 12

WAR DIARY

FOR

DECEMBER 1916

12D
5 Sheets

Army Form C. 2118

WAR DIARY
or
INTELLIGENCE SUMMARY

(Erase heading not required.)

Instructions regarding War Diaries and Intelligence Summaries are contained in F. S. Regs., Part II. and the Staff Manual respectively. Title Pages will be prepared in manuscript.

Place	Date	Hour	Summary of Events and Information	Remarks and references to Appendices
			CONFIDENTIAL. WAR DIARY of 15th Battalion R. W. F. (London Welsh) From 1st December 1916. To 31st December 1916 Volume XII	

C. C. Norman Lt Col
~~[illegible]~~ Comd 15th Bn RWF

1875 Wt. W593/826 1,000,000 4/15 J.B.C. & A. A.D.S.S./Forms/C. 2118.

WAR DIARY
or
INTELLIGENCE SUMMARY.
(Erase heading not required.)

Instructions regarding War Diaries and Intelligence Summaries are contained in F. S. Regs., Part II. and the Staff Manual respectively. Title pages will be prepared in manuscript.

Army Form C. 2118.

Place	Date	Hour	Summary of Events and Information	Remarks and references to Appendices
Ypres ELVERDINGHE SECTOR.	1·12·16.		Relieved by the 16th Battalion R.W.F. in Front Line. Relief complete 6·30 p.m.	
	2nd.		In Support along West of CANAL BANK. Enemy after heavy bombardment commencing at 12 midnight until 1. A.M. raided front Line, taking one Officer and one O.R. prisoners of the 16th Batt. R.W.F. Our casualties two OR wounded (one remained at duty) and one OR Killed.	
	3		In Support.	
	4.		Relieved the 16th Battalion R.W.F. in Front Line Relief complete 6·45 p.m.	
	5		In front Line	
	6.		" " "	
	7.		Relieved by the 16th Battalion R.W.F. Relief complete 6·30 p.m.	
	8.		In Support. West of YSER CANAL BANK.	
	9.		" "	
	10.		Relieved the 16th Battalion R.W.F. in Front Line, Relief complete. 6·30 p.m.	
	11.		Front Line.	
	12		" "	
	13.		Relieved by 16th Battalion Rifle Brigade 39th Division in Front Line. Relief Complete 2·30 p.m.	

T2134. Wt. W708–776. 500000. 4/15. Sir J. C. & S.

Instructions regarding War Diaries and Intelligence Summaries are contained in F. S. Regs., Part II. and the Staff Manual respectively. Title pages will be prepared in manuscript.

WAR DIARY
or
INTELLIGENCE SUMMARY.
(Erase heading not required.)

Army Form C. 2118.

Place	Date	Hour	Summary of Events and Information	Remarks and references to Appendices
Ypres. Elverdinghe Sector.			Battalion staying on West of YSER CANAL BANK until relieved by the 1st Cambridgeshire Regiment at 7.45 p.m. when the Battalion proceeded to Poperinghe by train from Ypres Asylum at 10.0 p.m. arriving at Poperinghe at 11.30 p.m. Spent remainder of night at Poperinghe	
BOLLEZEELE.	14.		Left Poperinghe (Cheesemarket Station) at 10.0 a.m. arriving Bollezeele at 12.30 p.m.	
	15		Training at BOLLEZEELE.	
	16			
	17			
	18			
	19		Battalion inspected by General Officer, Commander in Chief Sir Douglas Haig. G.C.B. G.C.V.O. K.C.I.E. a.B.C.	
	20		Training	
	21		" "	
	22		" "	

T2134. Wt. W708–776. 500000. 4/15. Sir J. C. & S.

Instructions regarding War Diaries and Intelligence Summaries are contained in F. S. Regs., Part II. and the Staff Manual respectively. Title pages will be prepared in manuscript.

WAR DIARY
or
INTELLIGENCE SUMMARY.
(*Erase heading not required.*)

Army Form C. 2118.

Place	Date	Hour	Summary of Events and Information	Remarks and references to Appendices
BOLLEZEELE.	23.		Training	
	24		Do	
	25		"	
	26		"	
	27		"	
	28		"	
	29		"	
	30		Proceeded to Camp E. to be attached to 39th Division for work and training. Entrained at BOLLEZEELE at 11.17 a.m. arriving at 4.0 p.m. at Camp E.	
	31.		B. C & D Companies proceeded to Elverdinghe for work (Cable burying). under direction of 39th Division. A. Coy. remaining at Camp E for training	

A Norman Lt Col
~~W. [illegible] Lt Col~~
Comdg 15th R Bn RWK

WAR DIARY

Vol 13

FOR

JANUARY 1917

15th BATT: ROYAL WELSH FUSILIERS

Instructions regarding War Diaries and Intelligence Summaries are contained in F. S. Regs., Part II. and the Staff Manual respectively. Title pages will be prepared in manuscript.

WAR DIARY
or
INTELLIGENCE SUMMARY.
(Erase heading not required.)

Army Form C. 2118.

Place	Date	Hour	Summary of Events and Information	Remarks and references to Appendices
			CONFIDENTIAL WAR DIARY of 15th BATTALION RWF (LONDON WELSH) From January 1st 1914 To January 31st 1914 VOLUME XIII.	

T2134. Wt. W708-776. 500000. 4/15. Sir J. C. & S.

WAR DIARY
or
INTELLIGENCE SUMMARY.

(Erase heading not required.)

Instructions regarding War Diaries and Intelligence Summaries are contained in F. S. Regs., Part II. and the Staff Manual respectively. Title pages will be prepared in manuscript.

Army Form C. 2118.

Place	Date	Hour	Summary of Events and Information	Remarks and references to Appendices
	1917			
	Jan 1 & 13		B. C. & D Coys at ELVERDINGHE cable burying under direction of 39th Division	
			A Coy in 'E' Camp training	
YPRES. LANCASHIRE FARM SECTOR	Jan 14		Battalion relieved 14th Battn K.R.R. (39th Division) on CANAL BANK	
			Support Area, Relief complete 6.20 pm	
	" 15		In Support, CANAL BANK	
	" 16		—— do ——	
	" 17		—— do ——	
	" 18		Relieved 16th Battn R.W.F. in Front Line. Relief complete 6-0 pm.	
	" 19		Front Line. Casualties 1 OR Wounded	
	" 20		" " " 3 OR "	
	" 21		" " " 2 OR "	
	" 22		" " " 2 OR Killed 1 OR. wounded. Relieved by	
			16th Battn R.W.F. relief complete 7.15 pm.	
	23		In Support, CANAL BANK.	
	24		—— do ——	
	25		—— do ——	

T2134. Wt. W708-776. 500000. 4/15. Sir J. C. & S.

Instructions regarding War Diaries and Intelligence Summaries are contained in F. S. Regs., Part II. and the Staff Manual respectively. Title pages will be prepared in manuscript.

WAR DIARY or INTELLIGENCE SUMMARY.

(Erase heading not required.)

Army Form C. 2118.

Place	Date	Hour	Summary of Events and Information	Remarks and references to Appendices
YPRES LANCASHIRE FARM SECTOR	1914			
	Jan	26	Relieved 16th Battn RWF in Front Line. Relief Complete 6.40 pm	
		27	In Front Line	
		28	— do —	
		29	— do —	
		30	— do — Relieved by 16th Battn RWF Relief complete 6.25 pm. On relief 3 Coys returned to CANAL BANK, and B Coy to POPERINGHE for 2 days rest.	
		31	In Support. Canal Bank	
—	Nov 25 to Jan 31		} Lt Col Venables Llewellyn 2nd Glam Yeomanry attached to Battalion for Instruction	
	Jan 25.		Major E. J. Penthery O Kelly R.W.F. from 39th Divisional H'Qts attached for Instruction	
			New Year Honours List	
			Lt Col R.C. Bell (C.L.H) D.S.O	
			No 21549 Coy Sergt Major H C Ford Military Cross	
			Capt H.V. Williams mentioned in Despatches	
			No 22680 Pte W. T. Saterlay mentioned in Despatches.	C. Chapman Lt Col Comdg 15th RWF

T2134. Wt. W708—776. 500000. 4/15. Sir J. C. & S.

Vol 14

WAR DIARY

15th BATTn R.W.F.

FEBRUARY 1917

Instructions regarding War Diaries and Intelligence Summaries are contained in F. S. Regs., Part II. and the Staff Manual respectively. Title pages will be prepared in manuscript.

WAR DIARY
or
INTELLIGENCE SUMMARY.

(*Erase heading not required.*)

Army Form C. 2118.

Place	Date	Hour	Summary of Events and Information	Remarks and references to Appendices

Confidential

War Diary

of

15th Battalion R. W. F.

(London Welsh)

From February 1st 1917 To February 28th 1917

Volume XIV

T2134. Wt. W708–776. 500000. 4/15. Sir J. C. & S.

Instructions regarding War Diaries and Intelligence Summaries are contained in F. S. Regs., Part II. and the Staff Manual respectively. Title pages will be prepared in manuscript.

WAR DIARY
or
INTELLIGENCE SUMMARY.
(Erase heading not required.)

Army Form C. 2118.

Place	Date	Hour	Summary of Events and Information	Remarks and references to Appendices
W of YSER Canal Bank, due E of BRIELEN	Feb 1	.	Battalion in reserve along W Canal Bank to 16th RWF. The cold spell which set in during mid-January continues; ground is therefore frozen, also the Canal. Our bombers keep the ice broken on the Canal by bombing nightly. All work is hampered; digging is out of the question, except where RE's first blow up the surface soil.	
			Strength of battalion in the trenches & First-line Transport 486 officers & men.	
			During day BOESINGHE sector on our left bombarded by Corps Heavy Artillery. Some retaliation along Canal Bank, but no casualties in this unit	
"	2.		Much artillery activity on both sides, & a great concentration of guns proceeding behind us for a suspected enemy attack.	
			Twelve men wounded during one of the bombardments (two since died of wounds)	
"	3.	12 noon	Battalion H.Q. bombarded for 20 minutes } no losses, although shells of 5.9 & 4.2	
		5.30	" " " " 30 " } HE & Shrapnel, were used	
		6.20 pm	We relieved 16th RWF in the front line	
	4.		Cases of 'Trench' Feet reappear, probably on account of the extreme cold which continues. Every precaution laid down from Above is being taken. The	

T2134. Wt. W708—776. 500000. 4/15. Sir J. C. & S.

2

WAR DIARY
or
INTELLIGENCE SUMMARY.
(*Erase heading not required.*)

Army Form C. 2118.

Instructions regarding War Diaries and Intelligence Summaries are contained in F. S. Regs., Part II. and the Staff Manual respectively. Title pages will be prepared in manuscript.

Place	Date	Hour	Summary of Events and Information	Remarks and references to Appendices
			Term 'Trench' foot probably a misnomer as reinforcements have been known to contract it in cold trucks & A.S.C. drivers on their G.S. Wagons.	
			Conditions during the day very misty; guns are quiet; men & officers roam about overland routes	
"	5		Misty again & therefore quiet. A wire from Brigade announcing a rupture in the diplomatic relations of U.S.A. & Germany enlivens our interest in things generally & causes us to speculate brilliantly on the future – generally agreed that Wilson would rather have written another note, had he not exhausted his [illegible].	
	6.		A day of bombardments, which provoked severe retaliation on the Canal Bank. 2 Lt Owen Jones wounded by Shrapnel on Canal Bank	
		5pm	Enemy opened intense artillery fire on the whole front line; happily it lasted but 10 minutes, & there were no casualties.	
	7.		Artillery activity continues; our casualties 1 man killed, 3 wounded.	
			Frost also continues; ice over 1 ft thick on the Canal; cases of trench feet disappearing – hints that present organisation & vigilance has defeated the complaint	
	8		Battalion relieved in front line by 16 R.W.F. 'A' Coy proceeded to Poperinghe to rest for 2 days	

T2134. Wt. W708–776. 500000. 4/15. Sir J. C. & S.

3

Instructions regarding War Diaries and Intelligence Summaries are contained in F. S. Regs., Part II. and the Staff Manual respectively. Title pages will be prepared in manuscript.

WAR DIARY
or
INTELLIGENCE SUMMARY.

(Erase heading not required.)

Army Form C. 2118.

Place	Date	Hour	Summary of Events and Information	Remarks and references to Appendices
"	8		Frost continuing; artillery active. Constantly meeting strange gunners in the line (being from the Mobile Brigades of other Divisions in the Second Army) – all in dreadful earnest about an impending enemy attack	
	9		Heavy bombardment of enemy lines opposite the Divn on our Right; not altogether quiet on our sector	
	10.		Lt Col Norman leaves for Second Army School – 6 days course & Battalion commanded by Major E Davies	
	11.		Wire from Brigade announces that CROIX DE GUERRE is conferred on No 25901 Sergt Edward Lewis of 'B' Coy. This NCO has been three times wounded with the unit when wiring in front of our line – a curious fellow who is never happy unless wiring.	
			Battalion relieve 16 RWF in front line	
	12	"	Thaw setting in, but very gradual	
		5.15pm	Intense Bombardment of Canal Bk for 15 minutes – no casualties	
			Right Front Coy also bombarded during the night; no enemy raid follows	
	13		Thaw continuing: no incident of note. A return from Companies showed that the Battalion had caught 342 rats in traps since Feb 1st – the first	

T2134. Wt. W708–776. 500000. 4/15. Sir J. C. & S.

4

WAR DIARY
or
INTELLIGENCE SUMMARY.
(Erase heading not required.)

Instructions regarding War Diaries and Intelligence Summaries are contained in F. S. Regs., Part II. and the Staff Manual respectively. Title pages will be prepared in manuscript.

Army Form C. 2118.

Place	Date	Hour	Summary of Events and Information	Remarks and references to Appendices
			has probably killed more..!	
	14		A most impressive crusade against 'TINS' organised & over 600 sandbags full collected. Yet this has made no impression on them & every shell unearths more.	
	15	·	Misty. Battalion relieved by 16 RWF. D Coy proceeds to Poperinghe for 2 days rest.	
	16		Thaw becoming more marked, & our men are able to show more progress with work. Dug out accommodation in Front & Support lines is being vastly improved	
	17		A solitary 18 pounder has apparently been brought close up (RIVOLI Farm), & is cutting wire for 14th RWF raid tonight; this gun is not molested by the enemy	
	18	3 am.	14th RWF raid enemy trenches - unsuccessful, as the enemy was prepared for it	
	19		Battalion relieves 16 RWF in front line. Weather now almost mild & slightly damp. A relief suspected opposite us (18th Res Divn relieving 17th Res Divn) & not yet confirmed	
			Battalion HdQtrs again bombarded for 20 minutes, no casualties	
	20		Quiet. Thanks to [illegible] 16th an almost imperceptible thaw, the trenches are not giving extra trouble	
	21		"	
	22		"	

T2134. Wt. W708-776. 500000. 4/15. Sir J. C. & S.

5

Instructions regarding War Diaries and Intelligence Summaries are contained in F. S. Regs., Part II. and the Staff Manual respectively. Title pages will be prepared in manuscript.

WAR DIARY
or
INTELLIGENCE SUMMARY.
(*Erase heading not required.*)

Army Form C. 2118.

Place	Date	Hour	Summary of Events and Information	Remarks and references to Appendices
	23		Battalion relieved by 16 RWF. Early in the morning, before relief one of our fighting patrols under 2/Lt A.T. Williams dispersed an enemy patrol — this being the only instance of the enemy being discovered in No Man's Land during the month by our patrols.	
	24.		Quiet; the guns which concentrated behind us are vanishing, so we are resuming normal conditions	
	25	3am	Enemy Raided 14th RWF on our right; casualties rather severe; we sustained none.	
	26		Quiet	
	27		Relieved 16 RWF in front line; no incident	
	28.		Misty & Quiet	

[illegible]

T2134. Wt. W708–776. 500000. 4/15. Sir J. C. & S.

15th BATT. ROYAL WELSH FUSILIERS

Vol 15

WAR DIARY

FOR

MARCH 1917

Instructions regarding War Diaries and Intelligence Summaries are contained in F. S. Regs., Part II. and the Staff Manual respectively. Title pages will be prepared in manuscript.

WAR DIARY
or
INTELLIGENCE SUMMARY.
(*Erase heading not required.*)

Army Form C. 2118.

Place	Date	Hour	Summary of Events and Information	Remarks and references to Appendices
			Confidential War Dairy. of 15th Battalion R.W.F. (London Welsh) From. March 1st 1917 To. March 31st 1917 Volume XV.	

T2134. Wt. W708–776. 500000. 4/15. Sir J. C. & S.

Instructions regarding War Diaries and Intelligence Summaries are contained in F. S. Regs., Part II. and the Staff Manual respectively. Title pages will be prepared in manuscript.

WAR DIARY
or
INTELLIGENCE SUMMARY.
(*Erase heading not required.*)

Army Form C. 2118.

Place	Date	Hour	Summary of Events and Information	Remarks and references to Appendices
	1917			
W of YSER CANAL BANK E. of BRIELEN	1.3.17 to 3.3.17		Battalion in Front Line. During this period an exceptionally quiet time was experienced.	
	3.3.17		Relieved in Front Line by 16th Battalion Royal Welsh Fusiliers. Relief complete 4-0 pm.	
	4.3.17 to 7.3.17		Battalion in Support on CANAL BANK, during which time Working Parties were found for Canal Bank Defences, and Front Line.	
	7.3.17		Battalion relieved 16th Battalion in Front Line. Lt Col C.C. Norman returned to Battalion from leave.	
	8.3.17		Battalion in Front Line	
	9.3.17		do do do	
	10.3.17		Battalion relieved in Front Line by 16th Battalion RWF, and relieved in Support by 13th Battalion R.W.F. This was the first time the 13th Battalion had been in this sector of YPRES and this was owing to a re-distribution of the Line held by the Division. Battalion on relief in Support proceeded to 'E' Camp in Divisional	

T2134. Wt. W708-776. 500000. 4/15. Sir J. C. & S.

Army Form C. 2118.

Instructions regarding War Diaries and Intelligence Summaries are contained in F. S. Regs., Part II. and the Staff Manual respectively. Title pages will be prepared in manuscript.

WAR DIARY
or
INTELLIGENCE SUMMARY.

(Erase heading not required.)

Place	Date	Hour	Summary of Events and Information	Remarks and references to Appendices
'E' CAMP.	10.3.17.		Reserve, for Training and rest. Battalion arrived in 'E' Camp 9.30 pm.	
	11.3.17		The morning was spent in cleaning up, and in the afternoon a small aeroplane contact scheme was carried out, between the Signallers and the Royal Flying Corps.	
	12.3.17 to 18.3.17		Battalion training daily. Specialist classes were formed for the training of Lewis Gunners, Signallers, Bombers, Wiring. also firing on rifle ranges.	
	19.3.17.		The Brigade held some Recreational Training Contests, consisting of Relay Race, by Runners, Musketry, Bombing, Firing Rifle Grenades, Revolver Shooting, Gas Helmet race, and Cross Country run. The Battalion had as their opponents the 10th Battalion The Welsh Regiment. The following events were won by this unit:– Relay Race, Rifle Grenade Firing, Musketry, and Cross Country Run, also the 2nd prize in Revolver Shooting. Prizes were afterwards given by Brigadier General L Price Davies V.C. D.S.O. Commanding 113th	

T2134. Wt. W708–776. 500000. 4/15. Sir J. C. & S.

Instructions regarding War Diaries and Intelligence Summaries are contained in F. S. Regs., Part II. and the Staff Manual respectively. Title Pages will be prepared in manuscript.

WAR DIARY
or
INTELLIGENCE SUMMARY
(Erase heading not required.)

Army Form C. 2118

Place	Date	Hour	Summary of Events and Information	Remarks and references to Appendices
'E' Camp	19. 3. 17.		Infantry Brigade.	
	20. 3. 17.		Battalion under orders to proceed to line on 21st inst but at 6.30pm this was cancelled, orders being received that Battalion would proceed to BOLLEZEELE for additional rest and training. This order was subsequently changed, and the destination of the battalion was changed from BOLLEZEELE to MILLAM.	
	21. 3. 17		Battalion entrained at BRANDHOECK for ~~MILLAM~~ ESQUELBECQ and marched from there to billets at MILLAM, arriving at 6.45pm.	
	22. 3. 17		Battalion resting.	
	23. 3. 17 to 28. 3. 17		} Battalion in Training on VIII Corps Training area. During this period, the new organization and formation for attack as laid down in Official Publication S.S 143 dated February 1917 and issued by General Staff.	
	29. 3. 17.		Battalion left MILLAM for YPRES, marching from MILLAM at 1.30pm and entraining at ESQUELBECQ 5.30pm, arrived YPRES ASYLUM Station 9.30pm, where guides were met to conduct Companies to W. CANAL BANK (HILL TOP SECTOR) where battalion relieved 14th Battalion The Welsh Regiment, in Support position. Before leaving MILLAM billets were inspected by Corps Commander ~~Sir~~ Lieut General Sir Aylmer Hunter Weston K.C.B. D.S.O. Commanding VIII Corps.	

1875 Wt. W593/826 1,000,000 4/15 J.B.C. & A. A.D.S.S./Forms/C. 2118.

Army Form C. 2118

WAR DIARY
or
INTELLIGENCE SUMMARY
(Erase heading not required.)

Instructions regarding War Diaries and Intelligence Summaries are contained in F. S. Regs., Part II. and the Staff Manual respectively. Title Pages will be prepared in manuscript.

Place	Date	Hour	Summary of Events and Information	Remarks and references to Appendices
YPRES	31. 3. 17.		Battalion relieved 15th Battalion The Welsh Regiment. Relief Complete 9.50 pm	

Chandler Llewellyn
LIEUT.-COL.
COMMANDING 15TH BN. R. W. F.
(LONDON WELSH)

1875 Wt. W593/826 1,000,000 4/15 J.B.C. & A. A.D.S.S./Forms/C. 2118.

15th BATTN. ROYAL WELSH FUSILIERS. Vol 16

WAR DIARY

FOR

APRIL, 1917.

16 D
13 sheets

Army Form C. 2118.

Instructions regarding War Diaries and Intelligence Summaries are contained in F. S. Regs., Part II. and the Staff Manual respectively. Title pages will be prepared in manuscript.

WAR DIARY
or
INTELLIGENCE SUMMARY.

(Erase heading not required.)

Place	Date	Hour	Summary of Events and Information	Remarks and references to Appendices
			— Confidential —	
			War Diary	
			of	
			15th Battalion. R. W. F.	
			(London Welsh).	
			C. C. Norman LIEUT.-COL. COMMANDING 15TH BN. R. W. F. (LONDON WELSH).	
			From April 1st 1917. To April 30th 1917.	
			Volume XVI.	

2353 Wt. W2544/1454 700,000 5/15 D. D. & L. A.D.S.S./Forms/C. 2118.

Instructions regarding War Diaries and Intelligence Summaries are contained in F. S. Regs., Part II. and the Staff Manual respectively. Title pages will be prepared in manuscript.

WAR DIARY
or
INTELLIGENCE SUMMARY.
(Erase heading not required.)

Army Form C. 2118.

Place	Date	Hour	Summary of Events and Information	Remarks and references to Appendices
YPRES E. CANAL BANK.	April 1		Battalion in Front Line (Right Battalion, Right Brigade) 'A' & 'B' Coys supported by 'C' & 'D' Companies. Situation quiet. Nothing of note happened.	
	2		Inter-Company relief. 'C' & 'D' Companies in the Front Line, 'A' & 'B' Companies in Support. Relief reported complete at 10.10. pm. At 11.30 pm enemy bombarded our front for about half an hour with Trench Mortars, Aprx.Grid. V.E. & L.H.V. No. 9 & 10 Posts also TURCO FM [illegible] particular attention paid to them. HQrs Right Group were communicated with & retaliation obtained but after considerable delay. Our Casualties nil. Rest of night quiet	
	3		Heavy fall of snow commencing about 4.30 am. Morning quiet. Enemy bombarded vicinity of Front Line C.15.1 with .15 L.H.V. between 1 & 2 Pm. TURCO FM also lightly shelled. Visibility good, much activity on both sides in the air between 5 & 7 pm. By this time snow	

A6945 Wt. W11422/M1160 350,000 12/16 D. D. & L. Forms/C./2118/14.

Instructions regarding War Diaries and Intelligence Summaries are contained in F. S. Regs., Part II, and the Staff Manual respectively. Title pages will be prepared in manuscript.

WAR DIARY
or
INTELLIGENCE SUMMARY.
(Erase heading not required.)

Army Form C. 2118.

Place	Date	Hour	Summary of Events and Information	Remarks and references to Appendices
			Quite fine. Night quiet.	
	4th		FOCH FM shelled with 30 4.2's between 8 & 9 am. Morning wet but afternoon fine. Relieved by the 14th Batn R.W.F. in Front Line. Relief reported complete 10.15 P.m.	
	5th		In Reserve on the Canal Bank. Training carried out. Weather warm & fine. Situation quiet.	
	6th		Canal Bank. Training & work. Weather fine & bright. Aerial activity between 6 & 7 am. Enemy machines fired upon by our anti-aircraft guns. During afternoon enemy shelled LA BELLE ALLIANCE with about 40 4.2's. Damage slight. At night commencing about 9.30 pm enemy Machine Guns opened rapid fire & continued [illegible] to [illegible] spasmodically until after midnight. Battalion front on our right was subjected to heavy shelling & Trench Mortaring. Probable enemy raid.	

A6945 Wt. W11422/M1160 350,000 12/16 D. D. & L. Forms/C./2118/14.

Instructions regarding War Diaries and Intelligence Summaries are contained in F. S. Regs., Part II. and the Staff Manual respectively. Title pages will be prepared in manuscript.

WAR DIARY
or
INTELLIGENCE SUMMARY.
(*Erase heading not required.*)

Army Form C. 2118.

Place	Date	Hour	Summary of Events and Information	Remarks and references to Appendices
	7th		Canal Bank. Gas Alarm Test carried out commencing at 10.0 pm. Quite satisfactory. Weather bright, wind dangerous. Day very quiet. News received of formal declaration of war by U.S.A. on Germany. YPRES heavily shelled between the hours of 9.0 & 11.30 pm. What appeared to be a number of incendiary shells went with nice effect.	
	8th		Morning Quiet, fine & warm. At 11.45 am a German observation balloon was brought down in flames by one of our airmen. Later on in the day one of our aeroplanes was brought down with anti-aircraft fire. Shortly after reaching ground it was shelled by the enemy & set on fire. Relieved 14th Batn R.W.F. in the Front Line. Relief reported complete at 10.50 pm. Considerable M.G. (hostile) fire during night. Otherwise quiet.	
	9th		At 4 am Captain H.V. Williams O.C. 'D' Coy reported	

A6945 Wt. W11422/M1160 350,000 12/16 D. D. & L. Forms/C./2118/14.

Instructions regarding War Diaries and Intelligence Summaries are contained in F. S. Regs., Part II. and the Staff Manual respectively. Title pages will be prepared in manuscript.

WAR DIARY
or
INTELLIGENCE SUMMARY.
(Erase heading not required.)

Army Form C. 2118.

Place	Date	Hour	Summary of Events and Information	Remarks and references to Appendices
			that two Huns were seen inside our own wire between Posts 9 & 10. They were fired upon but got away leaving a cap, rifle, handkerchief & 5 stick-bombs behind. Heavy bombardment heard to the South of YPRES. The remainder of YPRES TOWER knocked down about 11 am (officially reported collapsed) during a bombardment. Dense clouds of yellow smoke lay about. At 5.10 pm 'R' Coy (Right Support) was shelled for 20 minutes with shrapnel & H.E. No damage or casualties. HILL TOP FM shelled at 8.45 pm with about 20 4.2's. One direct hit obtained on TUNNEL. Test Gas Alarm carried out at 9.30 pm. Owing to strong westerly wind blowing at the time it was impossible to hear the gas-gongs being sounded in the front line at Battn HQrs LA BELLE ALLIANCE. Weather much colder. Snow showers all day. Hostile M.G.'s active during the	

A6945 Wt. W11422/M1160 350,000 12/16 D. D. & L. Forms/C./2118/14.

Instructions regarding War Diaries and Intelligence Summaries are contained in F. S. Regs., Part II. and the Staff Manual respectively. Title pages will be prepared in manuscript.

WAR DIARY
or
INTELLIGENCE SUMMARY.
(Erase heading not required.)

Army Form C. 2118.

Place	Date	Hour	Summary of Events and Information	Remarks and references to Appendices
			night. 'C' Coy (Right front) shelled about 11.30 Pm. Three men killed + two wounded by Rifle grenades in Post 9. H.Qrs Right Group communicated with + quick retaliation given (in 3 minutes).	
	10th		Battalion relieved in LANCASHIRE FARM SECTOR by 15th Bath. The Welsh Regt. Relief commenced at 10.30 Pm and did not finish until 3.15 Am. On relief Battalion proceeded to W. CANAL BANK, CENTRE SECTOR (ZWANHOFF) in support position, relieving 10th Bath S.W.B.	
W. CANAL BANK.	11th		In support. Morning quiet. Strong wind, afternoon wet + wind dropped. Heavy snow-storm commenced at 5.15 Pm lasting until 7.30 Pm. Night quiet.	
	12th		About 10.30 Am three [illegible] sent over to W. YPERLEE Bank one killing a man at the baths. Day quiet + weather fine. About 11 Pm a heavy bombardment opened on the Belgian front. In all probability a	

A6945 Wt. W11422/M1160 350,000 12/16 D. D. & L. Forms/C./2118/14.

Instructions regarding War Diaries and Intelligence Summaries are contained in F. S. Regs., Part II. and the Staff Manual respectively. Title pages will be prepared in manuscript.

WAR DIARY
or
INTELLIGENCE SUMMARY.
(Erase heading not required.)

Army Form C. 2118.

Place	Date	Hour	Summary of Events and Information	Remarks and references to Appendices
			wind.	
	13th		Weather bright, situation quiet	
	14th		Weather fine & bright. Day very quiet. Relieved 14th Batt. R.W.F. in front line. 'A' & 'B' Coys front line, 'C' & 'D' Coys in support. Relief reported complete at 7.45 P.M. Test Gas Alarm was carried out quite satisfactorily at 10. P.M. Situation quiet.	
	15th		In front line. Situation quiet. Weather dull & wet. Belgian front heavily shelled during the afternoon. No aerial activity owing to high wind.	
	16th		Situation Quiet.	
	17th		Situation exceptionally Quiet. Weather wet & windy. Battalion relieved by 15th Batt. Welsh Regt. Battalion proceeded to ROUSSEL FM (B.13.a Central) for training, arriving 3.30 A.M.	
	18th		ROUSSEL FM. Snow & sleet.	

A6945 Wt. W11422/M1160 350,000 12/16 D. D. & L. Forms/C./2118/14.

Instructions regarding War Diaries and Intelligence Summaries are contained in F. S. Regs., Part II. and the Staff Manual respectively. Title pages will be prepared in manuscript.

WAR DIARY
or
INTELLIGENCE SUMMARY.
(*Erase heading not required.*)

Army Form C. 2118.

Place	Date	Hour	Summary of Events and Information	Remarks and references to Appendices
	19th		ROUSSEL FARM. Weather misty & wet. Baths & firing on Rifle Range.	
	20th		ROUSSEL FARM. Training.	
	21st		— do — Training. Weather fine but slightly misty.	
	22nd		— do — Weather cold & strong wind from N.N.W. Left billets at 9 pm & relieved the 15th Batn Welsh Regt. Relief reported complete at 12 midnight.	
	23rd		In Support in Canal Bank. Considerable aerial activity. Weather fine & warmer.	
	24th		In Support. Situation quiet. About 10 pm a heavy hostile bombardment commenced on Right Battalion front & spread along to the left. Battalion stood to in dug-outs. The S.O.S. signal was sent up both by the Right Battalion & the Left (14th R.W.F.) & our artillery opened fire almost immediately. Everything quietened down at about 10.45 pm & the Battalion stood down	

A6945 Wt. W11422/M1160 350,000 12/16 D. D. & L. Forms/C./2118/14.

Army Form C. 2118.

WAR DIARY
or
INTELLIGENCE SUMMARY.
(Erase heading not required.)

Instructions regarding War Diaries and Intelligence Summaries are contained in F. S. Regs., Part II. and the Staff Manual respectively. Title pages will be prepared in manuscript.

Place	Date	Hour	Summary of Events and Information	Remarks and references to Appendices
			at 11.0 p.m.	
	25th		In Support. Day & night generally quiet. Weather fine & warm.	
	26th		Quiet. Considerable aeroplane activity.	
	27th		Situation quiet. Enemy wire opposite our front was shelled from 9.30 am to 4 pm with 18-pounders & medium Trench Mortars. Artillery & M.G.'s fired during the night in bursts at enemy wire.	
	28th		A bombardment of concrete O.P.'s & M.G. emplacements in KRUPP SALIENT took place by 88th & 89th H.A. Groups with 6" & 8" Hows, from 10 am to 4 pm. About 3 pm enemy shelled COLNE VALLEY with 50 L.H.V. & 10 4.2's. Left Front Coy ('C') was not shelled during the day at all but at 12.30 p.m. an enemy trench mortar burst in No Man's Land between Posts 35 & 36. At 3.45 pm another fell in the same place.	

A6945 Wt. W11422/M1160 350,000 12/16 D. D. & L. Forms/C./2118/14.

Instructions regarding War Diaries and Intelligence Summaries are contained in F. S. Regs., Part II, and the Staff Manual respectively. Title pages will be prepared in manuscript.

WAR DIARY
or
INTELLIGENCE SUMMARY.
(*Erase heading not required.*)

Army Form C. 2118.

Place	Date	Hour	Summary of Events and Information	Remarks and references to Appendices
	29th		From 11.0 Am to 4 Pm there was heavy artillery bombardment of selected points in enemy lines & back areas. At 6.50 Am occasional H.E. was sent on to YORKSHIRE TRENCH & WHITE TR. by enemy. Early in the afternoon he retaliated to heavy bombardment with L.H.V's & shrapnel on WHITE TR & COLNE VALLEY. At 5.45 Pm three rifle-grenades fell to the left of Post-St. Weather fine & warm.	
			At 9.30 pm a Dummy Raid on C14a.3½ 4 was made. Enemy trenches were intensely bombarded by our Artillery. M.G.'s co-operated. Nearly ten minutes elapsed before the enemy put up the S.O.S by means of green rockets. Red & Golden Rain Very Lights were also used. Hostile retaliation was put on COLNE VALLEY, & BARNSLEY Rd. with L.H.V's & 4.2's. Front line ~~[illegible]~~ was also shelled. Everything was quiet at 10.25 P.m. We	

A6945 Wt. W11422/M1160 350,000 12/16 D. D. & L. Forms/C./2118/14.

Instructions regarding War Diaries and Intelligence Summaries are contained in F. S. Regs., Part II. and the Staff Manual respectively. Title pages will be prepared in manuscript.

WAR DIARY
or
INTELLIGENCE SUMMARY.

(Erase heading not required.)

Army Form C. 2118.

Place	Date	Hour	Summary of Events and Information	Remarks and references to Appendices
			had four casualties.	
			At 12.30 a.m. a raid was made by the Rifle Brigade under cover of an intense bombardment by artillery, Stokes fire & M.G. fire. The enemy retaliated on COLNE VALLEY & BARNSLEY with L.H.V's & 4.2's. Except for a little desultory shelling everything was quiet at 1.25 a.m. We had no casualties. Remainder of night quiet.	
	30th		Weather fine & warm. Situation quiet. Owing to excellent visibility there has been considerable aerial activity. The enemy has also carried out some counter-battery work during the day.	

A6945 Wt. W11422/M1160 350,000 12/16 D. D. & L. Forms/C./2118/14.

Vol 17

15th ROYAL WELSH FUSILIERS.

WAR DIARY.

FOR.

MAY 1917.

17D
9 sheets

Army Form C. 2118.

Instructions regarding War Diaries and Intelligence Summaries are contained in F. S. Regs., Part II. and the Staff Manual respectively. Title pages will be prepared in manuscript.

WAR DIARY
or
INTELLIGENCE SUMMARY.

(Erase heading not required.)

Place	Date	Hour	Summary of Events and Information	Remarks and references to Appendices
			CONFIDENTIAL. War Diary May 1917 15th Bn Royal Welch Fus C C Norman LIEUT.-COL. COMMANDING 15TH BN. R. W. F. (LONDON WELSH).	

2353 Wt. W2544/1454 700,000 5/15 D. D. & L. A.D.S.S./Forms/C. 2118.

Instructions regarding War Diaries and Intelligence Summaries are contained in F. S. Regs., Part II. and the Staff Manual respectively. Title pages will be prepared in manuscript.

WAR DIARY or ~~INTELLIGENCE SUMMARY.~~

(Erase heading not required.)

Army Form C. 2118.

Place	Date	Hour	Summary of Events and Information	Remarks and references to Appendices
CANAL BANK	1.V.17		The 15th Bn Rwlf having been relieved by the 14th Bn Rwlf in the left subsection on April 31st proceeded to CANAL BANK. The enemy shelled Bn area round about bridge 60 at 8.30am with HE. & at 8.50am the vicinity of Belmont Dump & railway line followed by shrapnel at 9.40am. Afternoon quiet, but the enemy renewed shelling of the bridges in the evening. Great air activity by both sides. WIND:- NE (wild) Weather fine & bright.	
do	2.V.17.		Very quiet day with the exception of a few rounds of shrapnel on FARGATE & CANAL BANK at 7am 8am & 9.30am. WIND:- NE. Weather fine.	
do	3.V.17.		Situation quiet. A few rounds of shrapnel were fired near Bridge 68. At 10pm the gas alarm & gongs were started & preparations were made against a gas attack which proved to be a false alarm. It was ascertained later that gas was discharged against the French at NIEUPORT. WIND:- E.N.E. Weather fine & bright.	
do.	4.V.17		The Bn relieved the 14th Bn Rwlf in front line & support left subsection. A & B Coys to front line. C & D Coys to support. Relief complete 9.30pm. Enemy shelled Railway & vicinity of BELMONT at 9pm. WIND:- N.W. Weather fine. Patrol commander 2/Lt. A. Trevor Williams	
FRONT LINE	5.V.17		Enemy shelled WHITE TRENCH & POST 32 with 77mm at 8.45am. BARNSLEY RD & COLNE VALLEY also received some attention. Rest of day quiet. Patrol Commander 2/Lt W. Macdonald. WIND:- E.N.E. Weather fine.	

2353 Wt. W2544/1454 700,000 5/15 D. D. & L. A.D.S.S./Forms/C. 2118.

Army Form C. 2118.

Instructions regarding War Diaries and Intelligence Summaries are contained in F. S. Regs., Part II. and the Staff Manual respectively. Title pages will be prepared in manuscript.

WAR DIARY
or
INTELLIGENCE SUMMARY.

(Erase heading not required.)

Place	Date	Hour	Summary of Events and Information	Remarks and references to Appendices
FRONT LINE	6.X.17		BARNSLEY RD. COLNE VALLEY & neighbouring trenches were subjected to a heavy bombardment from 2.35am to 2.55 am under cover of which a hostile raiding party entered our trenches at POST 28. Casualties 2 OR Killed; 3 OR wounded & 3 O.R. missing. The back areas were heavily shelled during the course of the day. Aeroplanes very active. Patrol commander 2/Lt. J.P. Lloyd. WIND East. Weather fine.	
do.	7.X.17		Situation quiet with exception of retaliation on the part of the enemy on COLNE VALLEY & CANAL BANK EAST at 6.25am. At night POSTS 32 & 33 received attention. Patrol commander 2/Lt. W.H. Griffith. WIND NE. Weather fine.	
do	8.X.17.		During the day the enemy shelled FARGATE & WHITE TRENCH (Junction of HARKNESS AV.) At noon 2/Lt. H.L. Wood was sniped & killed in POST 28. The Bn was relieved in the Left Subsection by the 14th Bn RWF, relief complete 10.40pm. Hostile aerial activity NIL. WIND - NE. Weather fine.	
CANAL BANK	9.X.17		A very quiet day. Five rounds shrapnel on East CANAL BANK at 9.35am. Back area in neighbourhood of DAWSONS CORNER shelled at in the evening. WIND - EAST. Weather fine & hot.	
do.	10.X.17		Enemy artillery was active at intervals throughout the day. CORRIDOR TRENCH, BRIDGE 6D, BUTT 22, FARGATE Strong Pt. HARKNESS AV. WHITE TR. & COLNE VALLEY all received attention in turn. WIND - East. Weather fine.	

2353 Wt. W2544/1454 700,000 5/15 D. D. & L. A.D.S.S./Forms/C. 2118.

Instructions regarding War Diaries and Intelligence Summaries are contained in F. S. Regs., Part II. and the Staff Manual respectively. Title pages will be prepared in manuscript.

WAR DIARY
or
~~INTELLIGENCE SUMMARY.~~

(*Erase heading not required.*)

Army Form C. 2118.

Place	Date	Hour	Summary of Events and Information	Remarks and references to Appendices
CANAL BANK	11.V.17		Another very quiet day on the Canal Bank. Hostile aeroplanes were rather more active than usual. WIND:- NE Weather fine + dry.	
do.	12.V.17		The enemy's artillery to make up for the previous day was very active. No shells fell on Canal Bank, but the front line + supports were shelled at intervals from 6.40 am till 6.15 pm. Our artillery replied. The Bn. relieved the 14th Bn R Ir F in the left subsection. C + D Coys to front line. A + B Coys to support. Relief complete at 9.45pm. Patrol Commander 2/Lt. O. Gibbins. WIND:- W.S.W. Weather fine + warm.	
do	13.V.17		Quiet during the day. Occasional H.E. on COLNE VALLEY. Our own artillery was especially quiet all day. Patrol commander 2/Lt. C Jones. WIND. S East. Weather fine + very hot.	
do.	14.V.17		Another raid, but not on our front. At 2.58am the enemy opened an intense bombardment on the whole Brigade front. The front line was subjected to heavy fire from T.M's Artillery + Rifle Grenades. At 3.20am our artillery commenced a splendid retaliation on S.O.S. lines which was kept up till after the enemy had ceased. A hostile raiding party which was observed behind our wire on the Right Bn front was engaged by Lewis Gun fire + prevented from entering our trenches. The party retired leaving 1 O.R. wounded in our wire. Our casualties (15th Bn R Ir F) through the bombardment were 3 O.R. killed + 5 O.R. wounded. Patrol commander 2/Lt. J.R. Williams. WIND:- West. Weather fine + warm.	

2353 Wt. W2544/1454 700,000 5/15 D. D. & L. A.D.S.S./Forms/C. 2118.

Instructions regarding War Diaries and Intelligence Summaries are contained in F. S. Regs., Part II. and the Staff Manual respectively. Title pages will be prepared in manuscript.

WAR DIARY
or
INTELLIGENCE SUMMARY.

(*Erase heading not required.*)

Army Form C. 2118.

Place	Date	Hour	Summary of Events and Information	Remarks and references to Appendices
FRONT LINE	15.V.17		Nothing of importance to report today in the front line. Support trenches were shelled slowly with 4.5 Cm. Between 6pm + 8pm the enemy persistently shelled a battery near DAWSONS CORNER causing it to retire. Our 'Hows' fired frequently during the day Patrol commander 2/Lt. F.L. Ratts. WIND:- NNE Weather fine + dry.	
do.	16.V.17		The first wet day for a fortnight in consequence of which there is nothing of import to report. Both sides artillery was very quiet. The only shelling of the day took place at 1.40 + 1.50pm when the enemy fired a few 77/mm towards BELMONT FARM + we directed a few H.E. on CANCER TR + PILCKEM VILLAGE. The 14th Bn RWF relieved the 15th Bn RWF in the front line Left Subsection + relief was completed by 9.40pm. WIND:- NNE. Weather wet + close	
CANAL BANK	17.V.17		The wet weather continues + working party tables not carried out. A fog hung about over the trenches for the greater part of the day. Initial preparations for Remove carried out. WIND:- NE. Weather wet + foggy.	
do.	18.V.17.		At 8am a few 77mm shells on COLNE VALLEY. Machine guns very active at dawn. CADDIE TR + SUPPORT shelled by our 18 pr. Afternoon quiet. The Bn. was relieved on CANAL BANK by 13th Bn The Welch Reg. Relief complete at 12.6am. Lt Col. C. Venables Llewelyn who had been attached to the Bn since NOV 1916 ordered to report to G.H.Q. for new appointment Weather fine + hot.	

2353 Wt. W2544/1454 700,000 5/15 D. D. & L. A.D.S.S./Forms/C. 2118.

Instructions regarding War Diaries and Intelligence Summaries are contained in F. S. Regs., Part II. and the Staff Manual respectively. Title pages will be prepared in manuscript.

WAR DIARY
or
INTELLIGENCE SUMMARY.
(*Erase heading not required.*)

Army Form C. 2118.

Place	Date	Hour	Summary of Events and Information	Remarks and references to Appendices
Z CAMP.	19.X.17		Having been relieved on CANAL BANK the Bn proceeded to YPRES ASYLUM STN & entrained to POPERINGHE thence marching to Z Camp on the POPERINGHE-WATOU RD reaching it at 4am. The move was resumed at 2.15pm when the Bn paraded & marched to HOUTERQUE which it reached at 4.15pm. Bn then proceeded to billets in neighbouring farms & rested for the rest of the day. Weather fine & bright	
HOUTKERQUE	20.X.17		Church parade in morning. Rest of day a holiday. Weather fine & bright	
do	21.X.17		Parades & training as per Battalion programme Weather fine & bright	
do	22.X.17		Training carried out as per programme. Platoon training in the morning. Battalion billets inspected by G.O.C. 113 Inf Bde. Weather fine & bright	
do	23.X.17		Parades & training very much the same as on previous day. Weather fine & bright.	

2353 Wt. W2544/1454 700,000 5/15 D. D. & L. A.D.S.S./Forms/C. 2118.

Instructions regarding War Diaries and Intelligence Summaries are contained in F. S. Regs., Part II. and the Staff Manual respectively. Title pages will be prepared in manuscript.

WAR DIARY
or
INTELLIGENCE SUMMARY.
(Erase heading not required.)

Army Form C. 2118.

Place	Date	Hour	Summary of Events and Information	Remarks and references to Appendices
HOUTKERQUE	24.V.17		Morning platoon training; afternoon route march under 2nd in command. Officers + N.C.Os carried out a scheme with aeroplane contact in afternoon. Weather fine + bright.	
do.	25.V.17		Parades + training as per programme. Weather fine + bright.	
do.	26.V.17		Parades as usual during the morning. Brigade sports held at HERZEELE in the afternoon. The 15th Bn Royal rather unlucky in several events. Weather fine + hot.	
do.	27.V.17		Church parade for whole Brigade on No3 Training ground. After service G.O.C. decorated several members of the Brigade but unfortunately none of the 15th Bn. Weather fine + bright	
do.	28.V.17		Training as per previous days. Nothing noteworthy to record. Weather fine + bright.	
do.	29.V.17		Training as per programme. Route march in afternoon. Weather fine + bright	

2353 Wt. W2544/1454 700,000 5/15 D. D. & L. A.D.S.S./Forms/C. 2118.

Instructions regarding War Diaries and Intelligence Summaries are contained in F. S. Regs., Part II. and the Staff Manual respectively. Title pages will be prepared in manuscript.

WAR DIARY
or
INTELLIGENCE SUMMARY.
(Erase heading not required.)

Army Form C. 2118.

Place	Date	Hour	Summary of Events and Information	Remarks and references to Appendices
OCHTEZEELE	30.V.17		The Bn paraded at HOUTKERQUE at 6am to march to OCHTEZEELE halting half way for breakfast. The march was accomplished in good time OCHTEZEELE being reached at 11.30am. The remainder of the day was set apart for rest. Weather dull with occasional bursts of sunshine.	
TATINGHEM	31.V.17		The Brigade march was resumed again at 6am. The Bn moved in splendid style reaching the goal – TATINGHEM at 11.45am. Billets were found in a rather dirty condition & a general clean up was organized. The remainder of the day was devoted to rest. Weather fine & bright.	

2353 Wt. W2544/1454 700,000 5/15 D. D. & L. A.D.S.S./Forms/C. 2118.

Vol 18

15th BATT. ROYAL WELSH FUSILIERS

WAR DIARY

FOR

JUNE 1917

18 D
10 sheets

Instructions regarding War Diaries and Intelligence Summaries are contained in F. S. Regs., Part II. and the Staff Manual respectively. Title pages will be prepared in manuscript.

WAR DIARY
or
INTELLIGENCE SUMMARY.
(Erase heading not required.)

Army Form C. 2118.

Place	Date	Hour	Summary of Events and Information	Remarks and references to Appendices
	JUNE			
TATINGHEM	1		Battalion at Tatinghem. In the morning A & B Coys fired on range on the training ground & C & D Coys in the afternoon. Baths at ST OMER during the day. Weather FINE	
do	2		Parades: Coy & Platoon Training, Baths at ST OMER. Night operations digging trench & wiring same etc (Consolidation Scheme) Weather - FINE	
do	3		Sunday. Church Parades in morning, rest in afternoon Weather - FINE	
do	4		Bn paraded on Training ground to practise the following. (a) The advance in two waves (b) The assault with Bayonet; dealing with enemy at close quarters (c) Forming up for trench to trench attack. Weather - FINE	

A6945 Wt. W11422/M1160 350,000 12/16 D. D. & L. Forms/C./2118/14.

Army Form C. 2118.

Instructions regarding War Diaries and Intelligence Summaries are contained in F. S. Regs., Part II. and the Staff Manual respectively. Title pages will be prepared in manuscript.

WAR DIARY
or
INTELLIGENCE SUMMARY.
(*Erase heading not required.*)

Place	Date	Hour	Summary of Events and Information	Remarks and references to Appendices
	JUNE			
TATINGHEM	5		Parades on training ground Practising an attack on a Strong Point Battalion Signal Scheme in the afternoon. Lt Col C C Norman 15th Bn RWF (London Welsh) awarded the D.S.O. Night operations; the attack in open country. Weather FINE	
do	6		Bn parade in morning without Lewis Gunners who fired on Rifle Range C A+B Coys in the morning; C+D Coys in the afternoon. Weather up to evening FINE, stormy later	
do	7		Parades as per programme on training ground in morning. Full Bn parade in afternoon for Gas Demonstration. Weather FINE	
do	8		Field training + field firing. FGCM held at Bn H.Q Weather - FINE	

A6945 Wt. W11422/M1160 350,000 12/16 D. D. & L. Forms/C./2118/14.

Instructions regarding War Diaries and Intelligence Summaries are contained in F. S. Regs., Part II, and the Staff Manual respectively. Title pages will be prepared in manuscript.

WAR DIARY
or
INTELLIGENCE ~~SUMMARY.~~

(*Erase heading not required.*)

Army Form C. 2118.

Place	Date	Hour	Summary of Events and Information	Remarks and references to Appendices
	JUNE			
TATINGHEM	9		Parades on training ground for attack practice + field work in general Weather - FINE	
"M" CAMP	10		Bn paraded at 8.30am to march to ST OMER where it entrained for POPERINGHE On arrival at POP. the Battalion marched to M Camp where it remained for the rest of the day. Weather - FINE but dull	
"M" CAMP	11		No parades except Bn Medical Inspection by Capt H B Day RAMC. At 8.30pm the Bn paraded to march to the line which was reached at midnight. Relieved 13th Bn WELSH Reg on CANAL BANK relief complete 12.50am. Weather - FINE WIND - SW	
CANAL BANK	12		On CANAL BANK till 6pm when 15th Bn RWF commenced to relieve 14th Bn WELSH Reg in front line. Relief complete 7.30pm. Weather - FINE WIND - SW	

A6945 Wt. W11422/M1160 350,000 12/16 D. D. & L. Forms/C./2118/14.

Instructions regarding War Diaries and Intelligence Summaries are contained in F. S. Regs., Part II, and the Staff Manual respectively. Title pages will be prepared in manuscript.

WAR DIARY
or
INTELLIGENCE SUMMARY.
(*Erase heading not required.*)

Army Form C. 2118.

Place	Date	Hour	Summary of Events and Information	Remarks and references to Appendices
	JUNE			
FRONT LINE	13		Bn in Front Line WHITE TR. BARNSLEY Rd COLNE VALLEY + FARGATE shelled with 10.5cm + 77mm at noon + CANAL BK. + Bn HQ from 3pm - 4pm. Weather - FINE. WIND - NNW. Patrol Commander 2/Lt E C D Radcliffe.	
do	14		The above mentioned trenches were again shelled with 10.5cm + 77mm at 12.20am + renewed with great intensity at 3.10am also on YORKSHIRE TR. + CANAL BK. between 9am + 10.30am occasional shells on FARGATE + round Bn H.Q. Afternoon quiet but at 9.40pm to 10.45pm heavy shelling of front line, supports + communication trenches very intense at 10.10pm. Weather - FINE WIND. NNW Patrol Commander 2/Lt. W.H. Griffith.	
do	15.		Repeated bombardment of front line at 2am. At 8.20am twelve 10.5cm shells on Yorkshire + HARKNESS TRS. During the day fairly quiet. Shelling renewed at 10.5pm on FRONT LINE. SUPPORTS + RESERVE positions. Casualties. 3 O.R. Killed. 9 O.R. Wounded. Weather - Wet. WIND. NNW Patrol Commander 2/Lt. W.H. Griffiths.	

A6945 Wt. W1144 22/M1160 . 350,000 12/16 D. D. & L. Forms/C./2118/14.

Army Form C. 2118.

Instructions regarding War Diaries and Intelligence Summaries are contained in F. S. Regs., Part II. and the Staff Manual respectively. Title pages will be prepared in manuscript.

WAR DIARY
or
INTELLIGENCE SUMMARY.
(Erase heading not required.)

Place	Date	Hour	Summary of Events and Information	Remarks and references to Appendices
	JUNE			
FRONT LINE	16		Day fairly quiet Bn relieved in front line by 14th Bn R.W.F relief complete 3.50pm. Weather - FINE WIND N.W.	
CANAL BANK	17.		Fairly quiet day, but in the evening enemy shelled CANAL BANK round Bn HQ Casualties 3 OR killed, 6 OR wounded Weather - FINE & dull Wind S.W.	
do	18		Light shelling during the day. Hostile aeroplanes active throughout the day, one brought down in flames behind CAESAR'S NOSE WEATHER - FINE. WIND. N.N.W. Patrol Commander 2/Lt W.H. Griffiths	
do	19.		At dawn, as usual, heavy shelling of CANAL BANK. Morning quiet occasional shelling in afternoon, heavy towards evening. CANAL BANK not the health resort it used to be no pyjamas while in reserve this spell in the line. Weather - FINE WIND N.W. Patrol Commander 2/Lt W.H. Griffiths	

A6945 Wt. W11422/M1160 350,000 12/16 D. D. & L. Forms/C./2118/14.

Instructions regarding War Diaries and Intelligence Summaries are contained in F. S. Regs., Par: II. and the Staff Manual respectively. Title pages will be prepared in manuscript.

WAR DIARY
or
INTELLIGENCE SUMMARY.
(Erase heading not required.)

Army Form C. 2118.

Place	Date	Hour	Summary of Events and Information	Remarks and references to Appendices
	JUNE			
CANAL BANK	20.		Enemy artillery active at intervals throughout the day. CANAL BANK again shelled at dawn. At 11.20, 12.10, & 1.40 pm this was renewed but did not delay relief of 14th Bn RWF in front line which was completed at 3.55 pm. Bn HQ again shelled from 9.15 pm till midnight.	
			Weather FINE. Wind N.N.W. Patrol Commander 2/Lt. W. H. Griffith	
FRONT LINE	21.		A fairly quiet day till 5.15 pm when COLNE VALLEY, BARNSLEY Rd. HARKNESS & WELSH HARP were shelled with 10 cm + 77 mm. Little damage caused.	
			At 11.30 pm under cover of artillery barrage forming box round C.Y.C. 55 Y5 + Stokes bombardment of CABLE + CACTUS TRS a party - No 13 Plt D Coy 15th RWF - entered the enemy trenches at C.Y.C. 55.Y5. The front line was found empty but the party penetrated to the second trench where a dug out was located occupied. The Germans within were called upon to surrender, but refused, throwing a bomb through the dug out door instead. Several bombs were thrown into the dug out by us till the place was a mass of smoke. In the fighting the Officer + Sgt in charge of the raid (2/Lt W.H. Griffiths + Sgt S. Williams)	

A6945 Wt. W11422/M1160 350,000 12/16 D. D. & L. Forms/C./2118/14.

WAR DIARY
or
INTELLIGENCE SUMMARY.
(Erase heading not required.)

Army Form C. 2118.

Instructions regarding War Diaries and Intelligence Summaries are contained in F. S. Regs., Part II. and the Staff Manual respectively. Title pages will be prepared in manuscript.

Place	Date	Hour	Summary of Events and Information	Remarks and references to Appendices
FRONT LINE	JUNE 21. (cont'd)		were wounded. On the sound of the ~~whistle~~ horn JE for the retirement being heard the men were faced with the problem of either entering the dugout to secure an identification or remove the wounded officer & Sgt. They elected to do the latter & unfortunately no identification were obtained. Nevertheless the raid was regarded as a great success. Weather FINE Wind NNW	
do	22.		Front was left alone today. Back areas shelled intermittently during the day. During the night BARNSLEY RD COLNE VALLEY WHITE TR. were shelled & a certain amount of damage to trenches & personnel was caused. Weather - FINE WIND NW. No patrol	
do	23.		A day of heavy shelling. The front line did not receive much attention, but the CANAL BANK was shelled from 7.15am to 2.30pm. Only slight damage was caused. This was renewed at night. Weather - FINE Wind SW. Patrol Commander 2/Lt. A.P.B. [illegible]	

A6945 Wt. W11422/M1160 350,000 12/16 D. D. & L. Forms/C./2118/14.

WAR DIARY

Place	Date		Summary of Events.
CANAL BANK	JUNE 24		Enemy artillery not so active as on previous days. CANAL BANKS EAST + WEST shelled during the evening the majority of which were "blind". Relieved in front line by 14th R.W.F relief complete 3.55pm Weather. Day fine turning to rain at night. Wind S.W.
do	25.		CANAL BANK shelled at dawn. Nothing to report during the day, but as darkness came on the roads + communication trenches were shelled. Great aerial activity. Weather - FINE. Wind S.W.
do	26.		At dawn as usual, CANAL BANK was again shelled, a great number of the shells being blind little damage was caused. At 1.15pm + 4.30pm shelling was renewed. Back areas received attention during the night. Weather FINE. WIND S.W.
do.	27.		A quiet day. The Bn was relieved by the 1st Border Regt. Relief complete 2.15am Weather FINE. WIND S.W.
TRANSPORT LINES	28		On completion of relief Bn proceeded to the Transport Lines where it remained during the day + night. Weather - WET. WIND S.W.

WAR DIARY

Place	Date	Summary of Events	Remarks
PRADELLES	JUNE 29	At 9am the Bn embussed at the Transport lines for Pradelles which was reached at 2.30pm, the Bn having had to march from CAESTRE the debussing point. The remainder of the day was set aside for rest. Weather FINE	
FLECHIN	30	Leaving PRADELLES at 6.30am by bus, the Bn arrived at its final destination – FLECHIN – at 11am. The billeting was not quite completed owing to the early arrival but everybody settled down by noon. Rest of day set aside for cleaning up billets & rest.	

J Edwards

MAJOR.
COMMANDING 15TH BN. R. W. F.
(LONDON WELSH).

Vol 19

15TH BN. ROYAL WELSH FUSILIERS

WAR DIARY

JULY - 1917

19 D
9 sheets

WAR DIARY FOR JULY

15th BATTN Royal Welsh Fus.

S. Ifor Williams Lt.
15th Bn RWF.

WAR DIARY for JULY.

Place	Date	Time	Information.
FLECHIN	1. VII. 1917.		Battalion paraded at full strength to march to training area. Morning spent in Battalion drill, afternoon in specialist training - each section in its own area. Weather fine + dry.
do.	2. VII. 1917.		Programme almost the same as previous day. Both morning + afternoon on training area devoted to Bn in attack. Weather dull.
do	3. VII. 1917		Baths given to Bn in the morning. Afternoon + evening Bn paraded by Coys to dig replica of German trenches on training ground. Last Coy arrived back at 7.45pm. Weather fine + dry.
do	4 VII. 1917		Morning very wet. Battalion paraded in Billets for lectures + specialist training. Bn paraded at noon to march to training ground for inspection by the Corps Commander. The Brigade was inspected at work over the trenches dug on the 3rd. Weather morning wet. later dry but dull.
do.	5. VII. 1917		The whole day on training ground; practise the advance over replica of trenches with barrage. Weather fine + bright.
do	6. VII. 1917.		Parades the same as on previous day. The attack again practised. Weather dull.

WAR DIARY. for JULY.

Place	Date	Time.	Information.
FLECHIN.	7.VII.1917		The Bn paraded at 6am for training on the Divl Training ground. The attack practised as a Division & witnessed by the Divisional Commander. Section training during afternoon. Weather fine.
do	8.VII.1917.		Church parades during the morning. rest & holiday in the afternoon. C.O. held an officers conference in the evening. Weather fine.
do	9.VII.1917.		Company parades outside billets both during morning & afternoon. Lectures on the attack & training "each section in its own area". Weather dull.
do.	10.VII.1917.		On training ground. Section drill & training in the morning. attack with barrage in the afternoon. Weather fine.
do.	11.VII.1917.		Training same as on previous day. Weather fine.
do	12.VII.1917.		No work carried out today. General holiday granted & much enjoyed by the men. Concert in the evening. Weather fine.

WAR DIARY for JULY.

Place	Date	Time.	Information.
FLECHIN.	13·VII·1917.		Parades inside billets owing to wet weather. Lectures + Specialist classes held both morning + afternoon. Weather wet + dull.
do.	14·VII·1917.		The Battalion proceeded to training ground + carried out the final practises of the attack over the trenches. Twice practised as a Brigade. Weather fine.
do.	15·VII·1917.		Company parades outside billets in the morning. Company training. Physical drill. etc. In afternoon Bn prepared to move which was to take place the following day. Weather fine.
STEENBECQUE	16·VII·1917.		The Bn paraded in the Square FLECHIN to march to STEENBECQUE at 5am; the latter village being reached about 1pm. Here billets were found + the remainder of the day devoted to rest. Weather fine.
ST SYLVESTRE CAPPEL	17·VII·1917.		The Bn paraded at 5am to continue its march to the forward area, arriving at ST SYLVESTRE CAPPEL about noon. where billets were found for the night. Weather fine.

WAR DIARY for JULY.

Place	Date	Time.	Information
"P6" PROVEN	18.VII.1917.		Bn paraded at 4am + marched to "P6" PROVEN area. Here tents were provided, pitched on arrival + a camp established for the night. Arrival at "P6" about noon. Weather dull + wet.
ST SIXTE AREA.	19.VII.1917.		Again on the move today. The Bn paraded at 9am to march to ST SIXTE where bivouacs which were provided were put up in a small wood. At 5pm Bn parade. A + B Coys under the C.O. to practise movements to be carried out in the daylight raid which was to take place by those two Coys. on the 23rd inst. C + D. Coys company training. Weather fine.
DUBLIN CAMP.	20.VII.1917.		Today proved to be the last day of the move. Bn paraded at 9am for DUBLIN CAMP which is situated on the WOESTEN ROAD + reached at 12 noon. Here we relieved the 1st Bn. S.W.B. No further parades ordered during the day. Weather fine.
do	21.VII.1917.		A day of rest. Bn paraded at 9am. A + B Coy practise raid. C + D. Coys section training + specialist work. Two hundred men away on fatigue. Weather fine.

WAR DIARY for JULY.

Place	Date	Time.	Information.
DUBLIN CAMP.	22·VII·1917.		Two working parties from C+D Coys had to be found today. Rest of Bn paraded at 9am for section training till 12 noon. 12 to 12·30pm lecture by C.O. to A+B Coys. outlining the plans + details for the daylight raid. Weather fine.
DUBLIN CAMP + CANAL BANK.	23·VII·1917.		Inspection parades during morning. Afternoon packing up + dumping of stores + packs ready for the line. At 6pm the Battalion paraded in fighting kit to march to Tugela Farm where the Bn assembly trenches for the offensive where to be dug. The trenches having been roughly marked out by the C.O + an advance party the work was proceeded with + three lines of trenches 4ft x 2ft at about 100yds distance were dug + camouflaged. Gas shells were sent over by the enemy during the night. Bn relieved the 16th Bn Rwf. in reserve. Relief complete 11.15pm. Weather fine.
CANAL BANK	24·VII·1917.		Various fatigues during the day. At 11·30am. CO's conference with officers of HQ. A+B. Coys to explain scheme + revised lines for the daylight raid. Several of Bn officers + men suffering from the effects of gas shells sent over the night before. Nearly all these were eye cases, the gas having got in + blinded the majority of the men. The 50% officers + men not going into action were sent down to Transport lines in the evening. Weather fine.

WAR DIARY for JULY.

Place	Date.	Time.	Information.
CANAL BANK	25.VII.1917.		At 9am the barrage opened for the raid; at 9.1am the raiders advanced towards the German trenches. Little opposition was encountered in the 1st line but the enemy were occupying the 2nd + the party returned leaving 2nd Lt. Lloyd + 15 O.R in the hands of the enemy. Weather morning wet. afternoon fine.
CANAL BANK	26.VII.1917.		Nothing of importance to record. Shelling less severe than on previous days. Gas shells discharged during the night. Weather dull
CANAL BANK	27.VII.1917.		Reports having been received from the RFC. that the enemy had withdrawn from the front + 2nd line of trenches. A Coy 15th RWF was ordered to push forward + reconnoitre. Unfortunately the reports proved false + the enemy were engaged in the 2nd line inflicting severe casualties on the Company. O.C. A.Coy. Major Evan Davies was wounded + taken prisoner as were a number of the N.C.O's + men. One platoon D Coy. in charge of an N.C.O. who went forward as support to A.Coy. were badly cut up. Weather fine.
do	28.VII.1917.		Bn in rest on CANAL BANK. Relieved during the night + proceeded to DUBLIN CAMP Weather fine.

WAR DIARY for JULY.

Place	Date.	Time.	Information
DUBLIN CAMP.	29.VII.1917.		The whole day devoted to rest + re-organization in readiness for the attack. Weather fine.
	30 + 31 VII. 1917.		Full details of these two days in next month's diary.

A. Ifor Williams
Lt.
15th Bn R.W.F.

Instructions regarding War Diaries and Intelligence Summaries are contained in F. S. Regs., Part II, and the Staff Manual respectively. Title pages will be prepared in manuscript.

WAR DIARY
or
~~INTELLIGENCE~~ SUMMARY.

(*Erase heading not required.*)

Army Form C. 2118.

Place	Date	Hour	Summary of Events and Information	Remarks and references to Appendices
FRONT LINE	27.VII.17		On the 27th July 1917 information was received that the enemy was falling back & the brigade was ordered to carry out a reconnaissance to ascertain if the information was correct. A. Coy. 15th Bn R.I.R. was entrusted with this duty. They went forward & reached almost to CACTUS JUNC, but met with considerable opposition & for the most part were either killed or wounded. Weather fine.	
DUBLIN CAMP	28.VII.17.		The Bn moved from the trenches to DUBLIN CAMP where a reorganization of the Bn was made by the C.O. The Bn remained in camp till the afternoon of the following day when it proceeded back to the line for the attack. Weather fine.	
do	29.VII.17.		Rest in Dublin camp during the day. The C.O. held a conference of officers & N.C.O's in the afternoon when the latest & revised details of the attack were fully explained to all concerned. Bn paraded at 7pm to march to ROUSELL FARM. Weather fine.	

A6945 Wt. W11422/M1160 350,000 12/16 D. D. & L. Forms/C./2118/14.

Instructions regarding War Diaries and Intelligence Summaries are contained in F. S. Regs., Part II. and the Staff Manual respectively. Title pages will be prepared in manuscript.

WAR DIARY
or
~~INTELLIGENCE SUMMARY~~
(Erase heading not required.)

Army Form C. 2118.

Place	Date	Hour	Summary of Events and Information	Remarks and references to Appendices
	30-VII-17		Bn rested during the day in camp + paraded at dusk to move into the assembly	
	+		trenches which were duly reached + entered without any eventful happenings.	
CANAL BK	31-VII-17		When in the trenches rations were issued out + a final conference was held	
			by the C.O. An officer was sent forward to CANAL BANK to report upon the state	
			of the Bridges so that the C.O. could determine by which bridge he would	
			lead the Bn across the CANAL. The reconnaissance sent forward reported that	
			most of the bridges were shattered but 6Z was still crossable.	
			The C.O. therefore led his battalion across 6Z bridge + by 2.30 am the	
			whole Bn was on E. CANAL BANK ready to advance + moved off soon after that	
			hour. The Bn objective was the Green Line having to pass over the 1st objective	
			(Blue Line) + 2nd objective (Black Line) before reaching its destination.	
			Zero was fixed for 3.50 am July 31st 1917, but it proved to be very	
			dark at that hour + great difficulty was experienced in keeping direction	
			in spite of the excellence of the barrage.	
			Once having got clear of CANAL BANK it was fairly easy going for	
			the Bn as far as PILCKEM where a German barrage was encountered + opposition met.	

A6945 Wt. W11422/M1160 350,000 12/16 D. D. & L. Forms/C./2118/14.

Instructions regarding War Diaries and Intelligence Summaries are contained in F. S. Regs., Part II. and the Staff Manual respectively. Title pages will be prepared in manuscript.

WAR DIARY
or
~~INTELLIGENCE SUMMARY.~~
(Erase heading not required.)

Army Form C. 2118.

Place	Date	Hour	Summary of Events and Information	Remarks and references to Appendices
Bn in attack	31-VII-17		with fire from machine guns + snipers. Naturally all this caused a few casualties but PILCKEM VILLAGE was passed with the Bn still in good formation. From the BLACK to the GREEN LINE the 15th R.W.F. supported by 2 Coys of the 16th R.W.F. + 6 Lewis guns from the 14th R.W.F. continued the advance to their objective. Considerable opposition was met with at BATTERY COPSE + by this time there were but few officers remaining. The Bn at this point got left behind by the barrage + the smoke barrage coming down on our leading lines tended to confuse the men. Many of the houses in BRIERLEY Rd were held by the enemy who fired from them. Just about this period Lt. Col. C.C. Norman OC. 15th Bn R.W.F. was wounded + ordered the Bn to consolidate on the IRON CROSS ridge. As no officers remained, the Bn was handed over to R.S.M. Jones who saw to the consolidation which was being carried out some way in rear of the GREEN LINE giving a greater task to the 115 Bde who were passing through us. This concluded the fighting for the Bn on the 31st of July + all that remained to do was to hang on to the position + beat back any counter attack which might be launched against them. Weather fine.	

A6945 Wt W11422/M1160 350,000 12/16 D. D. & L. Forms/C./2118/14.

113/38

Vol 20

15TH BATTN. ROYAL WELSH FUSILIERS

WAR DIARY

AUGUST - 1917

20 D
14 sheets

Instructions regarding War Diaries and Intelligence Summaries are contained in F. S. Regs., Part II. and the Staff Manual respectively. Title pages will be prepared in manuscript.

WAR DIARY
or
~~INTELLIGENCE SUMMARY~~.
(Erase heading not required.)

Army Form C. 2118.

Place	Date	Hour	Summary of Events and Information	Remarks and references to Appendices
			WAR DIARY	
			15th BATT ROYAL WELSH FUS	
			AUG 1917.	
			A. [illegible] Williams Lt. 15 Bn. R.W.F.	

A6945 Wt. W11422/M1160 350,000 12/16 D. D. & L. Forms/C./2118/14.

Instructions regarding War Diaries and Intelligence Summaries are contained in F. S. Regs., Part II. and the Staff Manual respectively. Title pages will be prepared in manuscript.

WAR DIARY
or
~~INTELLIGENCE SUMMARY~~.
(Erase heading not required.)

Army Form C. 2118.

Place	Date	Hour	Summary of Events and Information	Remarks and references to Appendices
IRON CROSS	1·VIII·17		The Bn remained on the IRON CROSS ridge during Aug 1st. On this day rain began to fall heavily putting the troops at a great disadvantage + adding greatly to their discomfort. At 3·10 pm news of a counter attack was received from the front + a heavy hostile barrage was put down on the STEENBEEK. However the Bn held its ground + nothing came of the counter attack.	
			At 9·45 pm the order was received that the Bn had to move up to the posts on the Green Line + about the same time the Bn was taken over by Capt. R. Bower. Weather wet + dull.	
GREEN LINE	2·VIII·17.		The relief was complete by about 1·30 am. At 2 am Capt. R Bower went round the outposts held by the Bn on the banks of the STEENBEEK + during his reconnaissance was hit by machine gun fire + taken to the rear. The Bn was then handed over to Capt. S.G. Fitzsimons who held command till the moment of relief. Weather wet.	

A6945 Wt. W11422/M1160 350,000 12/16 D. D. & L. Forms/C./2118/14.

Instructions regarding War Diaries and Intelligence Summaries are contained in F. S. Regs., Part II. and the Staff Manual respectively. Title pages will be prepared in manuscript.

WAR DIARY
or
~~INTELLIGENCE SUMMARY~~

(*Erase heading not required.*)

Army Form C. 2118.

Place	Date	Hour	Summary of Events and Information	Remarks and references to Appendices
STEENBEEK.	3.VIII.17		Rain again fell during the day turning the battle field into a sea of mud. A relief was expected, but did not take place. Nothing of importance took place & the Bn had to hold on to the outposts for another awful night. Weather wet.	
do	4.VIII.17		The rain again fell during the day, on the already tired out troops; but the relief expected the previous day took place today. Nothing further to report. Weather wet.	
ELVERDINGHE	5.VIII.17		The Bn was relieved by the 114 Brigade in the early hours of the morning & proceeded back to CANAL BANK. While the Bn was moving to CANALBANK Capt. S.G. Fitzsimons O.C. 16th Bn R.W.F. collapsed & 2/Lt Ratto took charge of the Bn. Motor busses met the troops on CANAL BANK & conveyed them to ELVERDINGHE CHATEAU where hot food & clean clothes were provided together with chocolate & cigarettes which were greatly appreciated by both officers & men. Rest in the chateau till evening when Bn paraded to entrain for Proven where it remained under canvas. Weather fine.	

A6945 Wt. W11422/M1160 350,000 12/16 D. D. & L. Forms/C./2118/14.

Instructions regarding War Diaries and Intelligence Summaries are contained in F. S. Regs., Part II. and the Staff Manual respectively. Title pages will be prepared in manuscript.

WAR DIARY
or
~~INTELLIGENCE SUMMARY~~
(*Erase heading not required.*)

Army Form C. 2118.

Place	Date	Hour	Summary of Events and Information	Remarks and references to Appendices
PROVEN.	6·VIII·17 7·VIII·17 8·VIII·17		On arrival at Proven the Bn was given three days complete rest. No parades took place with the exception of QM parades for the purpose of re-equipping the men. Weather during the three days stormy.	
do.	9·VIII·17		On the morning of the 9th Major R. H. Montgomery 13th Bn Welsh Reg. arrived to take over command of the Bn. Re-organisation parades in the morning; Kit inspection in the afternoon. Weather dull	
do.	10·VIII·17		Bn parades as usual with easy afternoon. Nothing of importance today. Weather fine.	
do	11·VIII·17		Bn parades during the morning – Bombing, Physical Training & Musketry. Half holiday in the afternoon. Weather fine.	
do.	12·VIII·17		Bn paraded for Church Parade which was held in PERSIA CAMP at 11am. Weather fine.	

A6945 Wt. W11422/M1160 350,000 12/16 D. D. & L. Forms/C./2118/14.

Instructions regarding War Diaries and Intelligence Summaries are contained in F. S. Regs., Part II. and the Staff Manual respectively. Title pages will be prepared in manuscript.

WAR DIARY
or
~~INTELLIGENCE SUMMARY.~~
(Erase heading not required.)

Army Form C. 2118.

Place	Date	Hour	Summary of Events and Information	Remarks and references to Appendices
PROVEN	13-VIII-17		Bn parades from 9am to 12 noon + from 2pm – 3pm. Physical Training Bayonet Fighting Gas masks drill carried out. A party of 25 OR per Coy paraded at 9.15 am for firing on the range at BOLLEZEELE. Lecture to Platoon Comrs by C.O. at 4.30pm. Weather fine.	
do.	14-VIII-17		Bn paraded in fighting order + marched to Training area where Bn in attack as per SS 143 was practised. Weather wet.	
do.	15-VIII-17		Parades again as usual during the morning with half holiday in the afternoon. Weather fine.	
do	16-VIII-17		In the morning the Bn paraded for Musketry, Bayonet Fighting + Extended order drill, route march in afternoon under R.S.M all officers on a tactical scheme under the C.O. Weather fine.	

A6945 Wt. W11422/M1160 350,000 12/16 D. D. & L. Forms/C./2118/14.

Instructions regarding War Diaries and Intelligence Summaries are contained in F. S. Regs., Part II. and the Staff Manual respectively. Title pages will be prepared in manuscript.

WAR DIARY
or
~~INTELLIGENCE SUMMARY~~.
(*Erase heading not required.*)

Army Form C. 2118.

Place	Date	Hour	Summary of Events and Information	Remarks and references to Appendices
PROVEN.	17-VIII-17		Bn parades during the morning: Gas drill in afternoon. The first list of awards for bravery in the field during the recent attack came to hand. 22995 Sgt A.E. Collins. 22257 Cpl E.H. Pritchard 56257. LCpl A.M. Williams 55137 " E.G. White. 21522 " I. Williams 22372. Pte J. Roberts. 53999 Pte J. Chapman 56123 Pte W. Shotton. all awarded the MILITARY MEDAL. Weather fine.	
do	18-VIII-17		The usual parades in the morning + afternoon. Bn parade at 5.30pm to march to PROVEN + entrain there for ELVERDINGHE where the night was spent at ROUSELL FARM Weather fine.	
ROUSELL FARM.	19-VIII-17		C.O's tactical scheme with the Brigadier in the morning also Church Parade on Bn parade ground. Move to LEIPSIG FARM at 2.30pm. On arrival at LEIPSIG FARM bivouacs were pitched for the night. Weather fine.	

A6945 Wt. W11422/M1160 350,000 12/16 D. D. & L. Forms/C./2118/14.

Instructions regarding War Diaries and Intelligence Summaries are contained in F. S. Regs., Part II. and the Staff Manual respectively. Title pages will be prepared in manuscript.

WAR DIARY
or
~~INTELLIGENCE SUMMARY~~.
(*Erase heading not required.*)

Army Form C. 2118.

Place	Date	Hour	Summary of Events and Information	Remarks and references to Appendices
LEIPSIG FARM	20.VIII.17		Protective trenches were dug during the morning. Parades for Musketry Bayonet Fighting + Specialist Training during the afternoon. At 8.30 pm hostile aeroplanes appeared overhead + dropped a bomb among the bivouacs killing 1 man + wounding 10. Weather fine.	
do	21.VIII.17		A+B Coys on the Rifle Range in the morning; C+D Coys in the afternoon. Nothing further to record today. Weather fine.	
do.	22.VIII.17		Bn parades at 9am + 2pm for the usual practices. The second list of awards received as under. Capt. H.B. Day RAMC " H.V. Williams O.C. D. Coy } MILITARY CROSS. 22002 L/Cpl W. Gysler AND 26559 Pte A Mayhill 22539 " A.E. Lewis AND 22035 " W. Mayhill } D.C.M. Weather fine.	

A6945 Wt. W11422/M1160 350,000 12/16 D. D. & L. Forms/C./2118/14.

Instructions regarding War Diaries and Intelligence Summaries are contained in F. S. Regs., Part II. and the Staff Manual respectively. Title pages will be prepared in manuscript.

WAR DIARY
or
~~INTELLIGENCE~~ SUMMARY.
(Erase heading not required.)

Army Form C. 2118.

Place	Date	Hour	Summary of Events and Information	Remarks and references to Appendices
LEIPSIG FARM	23·VIII·17.		Bn moved its camp into a field behind TALANA FARM. A hundred bivouac sheets + timber for same were drawn from R.E. at BARD CAUSEWAY DUMP + pitched by the Bn under a row of tall trees. No further parades but the day devoted to arrangement + pitching of the bivouacs. Weather fine.	
TALANA FARM	24·VIII·17		The usual programme of work carried out today. Nothing further to record. Weather fine.	
do	25·VIII·17		Bn paraded at 9.30am behind the bivouac field to receive the G.O.C. Brigade who came to present medals + certificates to those members of the Bn who had won them.	
			Distinguished Service Certificates were awarded to the following.	
			22478 Sgt. F.W. Tilling 22091. L'Sgt. J. Williams 22704 LCpl F.J. Dean	
			28124 L'Sgt. J. Coats. 22692 Cpl G. Humphreys. 21926 Pte A.J. Moore.	
			55906 Pte C.N. Baker.	
			Weather fine.	

A6945 Wt. W11422/M1160 350,000 12/16 D. D. & L. Forms/C./2118/14.

Instructions regarding War Diaries and Intelligence Summaries are contained in F. S. Regs., Part II. and the Staff Manual respectively. Title pages will be prepared in manuscript.

WAR DIARY
or
~~INTELLIGENCE SUMMARY.~~
(Erase heading not required.)

Army Form C. 2118.

Place	Date	Hour	Summary of Events and Information	Remarks and references to Appendices
TALANA FARM.	25.VIII.17	(Cont'd)	After the parade the Bn marched past the Brigade Staff dismissing afterwards for the morning.	
do.	26.VIII.17		Church Parade (Voluntary) at 11.30am. rest of day devoted to cleaning up. Weather fine.	
CANDLE TR.	27.VIII.17		The Bn relieved the 16th Bn Welsh Reg in reserve positions in CANDLE TRENCH & AY in the early hours of the morning. Bn HQ. proceeded to CANDLE TRENCH & all those N.C.O's & men not required in the trenches remained behind at TALANA FARM as it was thought that the Bn would be in reserve for one night only. This however did not prove to be the case. A reconnaissance was made by the C.O & other officers of H.Q. of the front line positions in front of LANGEMARCK. Weather wet.	
do.	28.VIII.17		Remaining in reserve. Nothing to record. Weather wet.	

A6945 Wt. W11422/M1160 350,000 12/16 D. D. & L. Forms/C./2118/14.

Instructions regarding War Diaries and Intelligence Summaries are contained in F. S. Regs., Part II, and the Staff Manual respectively. Title pages will be prepared in manuscript.

WAR DIARY
or
~~INTELLIGENCE SUMMARY~~.
(Erase heading not required.)

Army Form C. 2118.

Place	Date	Hour	Summary of Events and Information	Remarks and references to Appendices
CANDLE. Tr.	29.VIII.17		Bn still remained in reserve position. LANGEMARCK reconnoitred by O.C. Coys. Weather fine.	
do	30.VIII.17		Remaining in reserve position. Weather fine.	
do	31.VIII.17		Last day of our rest in reserve. Weather fine.	

A6945 Wt. W11422/M1160 350,000 12/16 D. D. & L. Forms/C./2118/14.

15th Batt. Royal Welsh Fusl[rs].

Vol 21

War Diary

for

September 1917.

Instructions regarding War Diaries and Intelligence Summaries are contained in F. S. Regs., Part II. and the Staff Manual respectively. Title pages will be prepared in manuscript.

WAR DIARY
or
INTELLIGENCE SUMMARY.
(*Erase heading not required.*)

Army Form C. 2118.

Place	Date	Hour	Summary of Events and Information	Remarks and references to Appendices
LANGEMARCK	1.IX.17	-	The Bn relieved the 14th Bn RWF in front line positions in front of LANGEMARCK during the night. Some shelling during relief otherwise nothing further to record	
do.	2.IX.17 to 4.IX.17		The Bn held the front line positions throughout the 2nd 3rd & 4th inst during which time casualties were slight & shelling at times fairly heavy. We were relieved on the night of the 4th inst by the 14th Bn Welsh Reg. After relief Bn proceeded to LEIPSIG FARM.	
LEIPSIG FM	5.IX.17		The Bn having arrived at LEIPSIG FARM at about 12 midnight, no parades were carried out today.	
do.	6.IX.17		Full parades. Physical Drill, Close Order Drill, etc carried out during morning. Range in the afternoon.	
do.	7.IX.17		Another full day. Musketry & Bayonet fighting in the morning, Arm drill & range in the afternoon. Cricket match played in the evening.	

A6945 Wt. W11422/M1160 350,000 12/16 D. D. & L. Forms/C./2118/14.

Instructions regarding War Diaries and Intelligence Summaries are contained in F. S. Regs., Part II. and the Staff Manual respectively. Title pages will be prepared in manuscript.

WAR DIARY
or
INTELLIGENCE SUMMARY.
(Erase heading not required.)

Army Form C. 2118.

Place	Date	Hour	Summary of Events and Information	Remarks and references to Appendices
LEIPSIG FM	8.IX.17		Parades as usual during the morning. Half holiday in the afternoon games played by the men. 21926 Pte A. J. Moore awarded the Military Medal for bravery shown on the Battle field of PILCKEM	
do.	9.IX.17		Church parades in morning. Brigadier General inspected billets & camp of Bn in the afternoon	
LEIPSIG FM SUEZ CAMP.	10.IX.17		The Bn was relieved in reserve position by the 12th Bn K.R.R.C & proceeded to rest in SUEZ CAMP where it remained for the next few days. Arrived at SUEZ CAMP at 12 midday & rested during afternoon	
SUEZ CAMP	11.IX.17.		A full days programme of training carried out together with baths at PROVEN. Brigadier inspected camp during afternoon & 50% NCOs & men sent to HERZEELE returned to the Bn.	

A6945 Wt. W11422/M1160 350,000 12/16 D. D. & L. Forms/C./2118/14.

Instructions regarding War Diaries and Intelligence Summaries are contained in F. S. Regs., Part II. and the Staff Manual respectively. Title pages will be prepared in manuscript.

WAR DIARY
or
INTELLIGENCE SUMMARY.

(*Erase heading not required.*)

Army Form C. 2118.

Place	Date	Hour	Summary of Events and Information	Remarks and references to Appendices
SUEZ CAMP	12.1.17		At 9am the Brigadier General Commanding presented to C Coy 15th Bn RIF the silver bugle won by that Coy in the Divisional Recreational Training scheme during the early months of the year. Full training programme carried out afterwards during morning & early afternoon. At 3.30pm football match v. 16th Bn RIF. Result draw 4-4 goals.	
do.	13.1.17		Training as per programme nothing of importance to record	
do.	14.1.17		Today the Brigade started the move into the XIth Corps area. The Bn paraded 10am & marched to ECKE where the night was spent.	
ECKE	15.1.17		The Bn resumed the march today & proceeded to the MORBECQUE AREA which was reached at about 1pm. Rest during afternoon.	
MORBECQUE AREA	16.1.17		Resumed the march and got as far as ESTAIRES where the night was spent. Arrived at ESTAIRES about 4.30pm.	

A6945 Wt. W11422/M1160 350,000 12/16 D. D. & L. Forms/C./2118/14.

Instructions regarding War Diaries and Intelligence Summaries are contained in F. S. Regs., Part II. and the Staff Manual respectively. Title pages will be prepared in manuscript.

WAR DIARY
or
INTELLIGENCE SUMMARY.
(*Erase heading not required.*)

Army Form C. 2118.

Place	Date	Hour	Summary of Events and Information	Remarks and references to Appendices
ESTAIRES	17/IX/17		Paraded at ESTAIRES at 10 am + marched to destination at ERQUINGHEM where Bn came into reserve positions for the BOIS GRENIER sector of the British front. Arrived in positions + relieved 2/5th Bn South Lancs. Relief complete 1.30pm	
ERQUINGHEM	18/IX/17		Parades round about billets during morning + afternoon.	
do	19/IX/17 to 25/IX/17		Bn in reserve position. Parades as per programme, football etc daily during period in reserve. Overland routes + tracks reconnoitred by all officers + district learned by officers + NCOs. On night of 25th the Bn proceeded to the front line where it relieved the 14th Bn R.W.F. in the Right Subsector. Relief complete at 10pm	
FRONT LINE	26/IX/17		Bn in front line. A Coy on the right B in centre + D on the left C Coy in reserve. Very quiet day. Nothing to report. Weather fine.	

A6945 Wt. W11422/M1160 350,000 12/16 D. D. & L. Forms/C./2118/14.

Instructions regarding War Diaries and Intelligence Summaries are contained in F. S. Regs., Part II, and the Staff Manual respectively. Title pages will be prepared in manuscript.

WAR DIARY
or
INTELLIGENCE SUMMARY.
(*Erase heading not required.*)

Army Form C. 2118.

Place	Date	Hour	Summary of Events and Information	Remarks and references to Appendices
FRONT LINE	27.IX.17		Another quiet day. A new HQ was started by Bn + work as handed over done by C Coy in reserve. Nothing of importance to report. Weather fine.	
do.	28.IX.17		Brigadier General inspected the front area held by the Bn during the morning. All quiet. Weather fine.	
do.	29.IX.17		The first bit of shelling experienced by the Bn while in this sector. Com-manders and Bn HQ shelled + parts of back area registered from 12-1.15pm. No casualties. Weather fine.	
do.	30.IX.17		A very quiet day. Nothing at all to report. Weather fine.	

R.H. Montgomery Lt Col
Comdg 15th RWF

A6945 Wt. W11422/M1160 350,000 12/16 D. D. & L. Forms/C./2118/14.

Vol 22

15TH BATT. ROYAL WELSH FUSILIERS.

WAR DIARY.

FOR

OCTOBER 1917.

22D
8 Sheets

Army Form C. 2118.

Instructions regarding War Diaries and Intelligence Summaries are contained in F. S. Regs., Part II. and the Staff Manual respectively. Title pages will be prepared in manuscript.

WAR DIARY

or

~~INTELLIGENCE SUMMARY.~~

(Erase heading not required.)

Place	Date	Hour	Summary of Events and Information	Remarks and references to Appendices
			WAR DIARY	
			FOR OCT. 1917	
			15th Bn ROYAL WELSH FUS	

A6945 Wt. W11422/M1160 350,000 12/16 D. D. & L. Forms/C./2118/14.

Instructions regarding War Diaries and Intelligence Summaries are contained in F. S. Regs., Part II. and the Staff Manual respectively. Title pages will be prepared in manuscript.

WAR DIARY
or
INTELLIGENCE SUMMARY.
(*Erase heading not required.*)

Army Form C. 2118.

Place	Date	Hour	Summary of Events and Information	Remarks and references to Appendices
Bois Grenier.	1.10.17		Battalion in the Front line. Except for aerial activity – everything very quiet. Weather fine	
do	2.10.17		A very quiet day. nothing at all to report – weather fine	
do	3.10.17		Battalion was relieved by the 14th R.W.F. ... Relief complete by 10 PM. Rain fell in the early morning & the rest of the day was very dull.	
Artillery Farm	4.10.17		Parades. Inspection of Arms & Equipment. – Weather wet & windy.	
do	5.10.17		Full parades, arm-drill, bombing, wiring, &c. carried out during the day – much aerial activity by the Enemy. & the shelling of back areas. Weather dull.	
do	6.10.17		Parades as yesterday. A very quiet day. Nothing to report Weather wet	
do	7.10.17		Church parades in the morning. Some aerial activity during the morning – otherwise – very quiet. Weather heavy rain fell all day.	

A6945 Wt. W11422/M1160 350,000 12/16 D. D. & L. Forms/C./2118/14.

Army Form C. 2118.

Instructions regarding War Diaries and Intelligence Summaries are contained in F. S. Regs., Part II. and the Staff Manual respectively. Title pages will be prepared in manuscript.

WAR DIARY
or
INTELLIGENCE SUMMARY.
(Erase heading not required.)

Place	Date	Hour	Summary of Events and Information	Remarks and references to Appendices
Artillery Farm	8.10.17		Bathing parades during the day. Weather wet. A Battalion runner was killed in billets by a dud anti-aircraft shell	
do.	9.10.17		Parades – Arm Drill, Wiring, bombing &c carried out during the day. Weather dull & wet.	
do	10.10.17		Parades as yesterday. A quiet day. Weather dull & wet	
do	11.10.17		Parades as yesterday in the morning. In the Evening the Battalion relieved the 14 RWFus in the front Line. "A" Coy on the right front. "B" Coy in the centre. "C" Coy on the ~~right~~ left front with "D" Coy in reserve. Relief complete by 7.45 pm	
Bois Grenier	12.10.17		In the front line. Some aerial activity. Trench Mortars "shoot" by the Enemy on our line. Our Artillery retaliated.	
do	13.10.17		Unit of the Portuguese Army were attached to us in the Line for instruction. Weather wet	
do	14.10.17		Considerable aerial Activity by the Enemy – Some artillery Activity otherwise very quiet.	

A6945 Wt. W11422/M1160 350,000 12/16 D. D. & L. Forms/C./2118/14.

Instructions regarding War Diaries and Intelligence Summaries are contained in F. S. Regs., Part II. and the Staff Manual respectively. Title pages will be prepared in manuscript.

WAR DIARY
or
INTELLIGENCE SUMMARY.
(Erase heading not required.)

Army Form C. 2118.

Place	Date	Hour	Summary of Events and Information	Remarks and references to Appendices
Bois Grenier	15.10.17		A very quiet day. – Nothing to report, weather fine but cloudy.	
do	16.10.17		Little to report. Some shells fell on the Subsidiary Line. one dropping close to "BHQ". Weather fine, The Portuguese troops finished their tour of instruction with us	
do	17.10.17		Artillery very active especially in the afternoon – Weather fine.	
do	18.10.17		Considerable aerial activity during day. – Artillery very active, Enemy used gas on our left. at about 10pm Weather dull.	
do	19.10.17		Artillery active on both sides Weather wet. Battalion was relieved by the 16th RWF in the Evening. Relief Complete by 8pm – without any unusual incident.	
Artillery Farm	20.10.17		Companies paraded for baths during the day Weather fine but dull.	
do.	21.10.17		Church Parades in the morning. Some Aerial & artillery Activity – Weather fine	
do	22.10.17		Full parades, Arm Drill, Physical Training, Wiring &c. Artillery fairly active, The Battalion played the 16 RWF at football in the afternoon	

A6945 Wt. W11422/M1160 350,000 12/16 D. D. & L. Forms/C./2118/14.

Army Form C. 2118.

Instructions regarding War Diaries and Intelligence Summaries are contained in F. S. Regs., Part II. and the Staff Manual respectively. Title pages will be prepared in manuscript.

WAR DIARY
or
INTELLIGENCE SUMMARY.
(Erase heading not required.)

Place	Date	Hour	Summary of Events and Information	Remarks and references to Appendices
Artillery Farm	22.10.17		and Lose, Weather fine, but dull.	
do	23.10.17		Parades as usual. Weather dull & misty. Battalion relieve the 14th R.W.Fus in the front line in the Evening. "D" Coy on the right front "B" Coy in the Centre. "C" Coy on the left front "A" Coy in reserve. Relief complete by 7.10 PM Enemy TM activity during night	
Bois Grenier	24.10.17		Some Aerial and Artillery activity during the day Weather fine.	
do	25.10.17		A very quiet day. Nothing of interest to report. Weather fine but dull.	
do.	26.10.17		Much Trench Mortar activity, & considerable liveliness by the Artillery during the night in consequence of a Raid carried out by the 10th Welsh. on our right. Weather wet.	
do	27.10.17		Some Aerial activity during the morning. Weather fine, but latter dull. In the evening the Battalion was relieved by the 14th RWF Relief complete by 7.30 PM During the day the Enemy shelled our battery positions in the vicinity of	

A6945 Wt. W11422/M1160 350,000 12/16 D. D. & L. Forms/C./2118/14.

Instructions regarding War Diaries and Intelligence Summaries are contained in F. S. Regs., Part II. and the Staff Manual respectively. Title pages will be prepared in manuscript.

WAR DIARY
or
INTELLIGENCE SUMMARY.
(*Erase heading not required.*)

Army Form C. 2118.

Place	Date	Hour	Summary of Events and Information	Remarks and references to Appendices
Bois Grenier	27.10.17 (Contd)		"Gris Pot" & "La Vesee"	
Artillery Farm	28.10.17		Church Parades in the morning. Some aerial and artillery activity during the day. Weather bright & clear.	
do	29.10.17		Companies paraded for baths. Enemy aeroplanes drop bombs on Baths causing one casualty in the 15" Bn. Some Artillery Activity. Weather fine	
do.	30.10.17		A very quiet day. Parades, – Arm drill, Wiring, Bombing, &c, during the day. Weather dull & very showery.	
do	31.10.17		Some Aerial Activity during the day. Artillery on both side active. Weather fine, & clear. The Battalion relieved the 14" RWF in the front line "D" Coy on the right, "A" Coy in the centre "C" Coy on the left & "B" Coy in reserve. Relief Complete by – 7.5PM	

R H Montgomery

LIEUT.-COL.
COMMANDING 15TH BN. R. W. F. (LONDON WELSH).

A6945 Wt. W11422/M1160 350,000 12/16 D. D. & L. Forms/C./2118/14.

Vol 2 & 3

15th BATT. ROYAL WELSH FUSILIERS

WAR DIARY

FOR

NOVEMBER 1917

E.M.

23 D
9 sheets

Instructions regarding War Diaries and Intelligence Summaries are contained in F. S. Regs., Part II. and the Staff Manual respectively. Title pages will be prepared in manuscript.

WAR DIARY
or
INTELLIGENCE SUMMARY.

(Erase heading not required.)

Army Form C. 2118.

Place	Date	Hour	Summary of Events and Information	Remarks and references to Appendices
			No 23.	
			WAR DIARY	
			NOVEMBER 1917	
			15th ROYAL WELSH FUS	
			Capt.	
			J Edwards Major Comdg 15 Regt	

A5834 Wt. W4973/M687 750,000 8/16 D. D. & L. Ltd. Forms/C.2118/13.

Army Form C. 2118.

WAR DIARY
or
INTELLIGENCE SUMMARY.
(Erase heading not required.)

Instructions regarding War Diaries and Intelligence Summaries are contained in F. S. Regs., Part II. and the Staff Manual respectively. Title pages will be prepared in manuscript.

Place	Date	Hour	Summary of Events and Information	Remarks and references to Appendices
BOIS GRENIER	1.11.17		Batt. in Line. A little Artillery activity during afternoon. Weather fine but dull.	
	2.11.17		Artillery very active all day. on both sides. Five rounds 4.2 gun. dropped on Subsidiary line in the vicinity of B HQ ~~[illegible]~~ destroying a dug-out; Weather. – Rain during afternoon + evening. very dark night.	
	3.11.17		During ~~the~~ morning. there was very little activity of any sort. Our heavies were active during the afternoon. Weather – dull & inclined to rain.	
	4.11.17		Very quiet day. The Battalion was relieved by the 14 RWF in the evening. Relief carried out without any noteworthy occurrence.	
Armentières Farm	5.11.17		Battalion in Reserve. Baths were allotted to Batt in the morning. parades as usual. Very quiet day. Weather – fine but dull.	

A5834 Wt. W4973/M687 750,000 8/16 D. D. & L. Ltd. Forms/C.2118/13.

Instructions regarding War Diaries and Intelligence Summaries are contained in F. S. Regs., Part II. and the Staff Manual respectively. Title pages will be prepared in manuscript.

WAR DIARY
or
INTELLIGENCE SUMMARY.
(Erase heading not required.)

Army Form C. 2118.

Place	Date	Hour	Summary of Events and Information	Remarks and references to Appendices
Artillery Fm.	6.11.17		At about 9 am an enemy plane came exceptionally low over our lines & succeeded in getting back to safety in spite of the efforts of our AA guns & machine-gun fire. Our "heavies" were active during the day. Baths for battalion in the afternoon. Weather very wet. Gas-Shells were sent over by the Enemy at about midnight, on our front, but their effect was not felt in the Reserve area. Alarm given, but no "stand-to"	
– do –	7.11.17		Usual parades. Very quiet day. Weather – wet & dull during morning but fine later.	
– do –	8.11.17		Enemy drops a few shells in the vicinity of "Artillery Farm" The Batt. relieved the 14 RWF in the front line in the evening. Relief complete without any unusual happenings. Dark & wet night.	
Bois Grenier	9.11.17		During the day the Enemy shelled our back areas round Bde HQ with heavy shells. Some aerial activity on both sides during the entire day. Weather fine but cloudy.	

A5834 Wt. W4973/M687 750,000 8/16 D. D. & L. Ltd. Forms/C.2118/13.

Army Form C. 2118.

WAR DIARY
or
INTELLIGENCE SUMMARY.
(Erase heading not required.)

Instructions regarding War Diaries and Intelligence Summaries are contained in F. S. Regs., Part II. and the Staff Manual respectively. Title pages will be prepared in manuscript.

Place	Date	Hour	Summary of Events and Information	Remarks and references to Appendices
Bois Grenier	10.11.17		Very quiet day Weather wet + dull.	
- do -	11.11.17		Aerial activity during the morning. A hostile plane dropped bombs in the neighbourhood of Subsidiary line. with little effect. Otherwise the day was fairly Quiet. Weather Showery.	
- do -	12.11.17		Quiet day. In the Evening the Battalion was relieved by the 14 RWF. During the night. the enemy. projected Gas on the 115 Bde. on our left	
Artillery Farm	13.11.17		The Battalion. paraded for baths at. Bac. St Maur. Artillery active during the day. Gas shells. sent over by the Enemy at midnight. Alarm Given + slight effect felt at Artillery Farm. Our Heavy Artillery retaliated a little.	
- do -	14.11.17		Usual parades. In the afternoon the Batt. played the RFA at football + lost. Concert in the Evening at Erquinghem Cinema which proved to be a great success. Little activity of any sort during the day. Weather fine but dull.	
- do -	15.11.17		Nothing to report. Weather fine + sunny.	
- do -	16.11.17		The Battalion relieve the 14 RWF in front line. Quiet night. Weather Showery. - fine night.	

A5834 Wt. W4973/M687 750,000 8/16 D. D. & L. Ltd. Forms/C.2118/13.

Instructions regarding War Diaries and Intelligence Summaries are contained in F. S. Regs., Part II. and the Staff Manual respectively. Title pages will be prepared in manuscript.

WAR DIARY
or
INTELLIGENCE SUMMARY.
(Erase heading not required.)

Army Form. C. 2118.

Place	Date	Hour	Summary of Events and Information	Remarks and references to Appendices
Bois Grenier	17.11.17		Battalion in line. Very quiet day. – Artillery very active during the night. Weather fine. but somewhat misty.	
– do –	18.11.17		Considerable T.M activity on the part of the Enemy during the afternoon. Our centre front being heavily mortared. Otherwise quiet. Very dark night causing considerable difficulty to the ration parties. etc. Weather very dull. all day.	
– do	19.11.17		Enemy again bombard our front & support lines with TM's in the later part of the day. Our heavies gave us some support. causing the enemy to cease fire.	
– do –	20.11.17		14 RWF relieve Battalion in front line. TMs again active.	
Artillery Farm	21.11.17		Very quiet day. Usual parades. Half the Battalion parade for the baths at Bac St. Maur. in the afternoon. Dull, wet day	
– do –	22.11.17		Remainder of Battalion go to baths in the morning. Usual parades. Quiet day. Weather fine all day. Battalion Concert in the evening at "Cinema" in Erquinghem.	
– do	23.11.17		The Enemy displayed considerable activity in the air all day. Weather dull.	

A5834 Wt. W4973/M687 750,000 8/16 D. D. & L. Ltd. Forms/C.2118/13.

Instructions regarding War Diaries and Intelligence Summaries are contained in F. S. Regs., Part II. and the Staff Manual respectively. Title pages will be prepared in manuscript.

WAR DIARY
or
INTELLIGENCE SUMMARY.
(Erase heading not required.)

Army Form C. 2118.

Place	Date	Hour	Summary of Events and Information	Remarks and references to Appendices
Artillery Farm	24 · 11 · 17		The Battalion relieved the 14th RWF in the Line. Portuguese troops in the Bde front for instruction. Great difficulty to find accommodation for the men at B.H.Q owing to the fact of the Portuguese using our dug-outs etc.	
Bois Grenier	25 · 11 · 17		Very little activity of any sort all day weather very cold & windy.	
– do –	26 · 11 · 17		Hostile TMs straff our centre & right Companies at mid-day. Causing one casualty in "B" Coy. Weather fine.	
– do –	27 · 11 · 17		Exceptionally quiet day. Weather wet & dull.	
– do –	28 · 11 · 17		The Enemy kept up a continual fire with 4·2s & 5·9s on our right & centre front & subport line almost all day. Our own artillery becoming very active in the afternoon. One man killed in "B" Coy. 14. RWF relieved the Battalion in the Evening. Battalion proceeded for one night only to Artillery Farm.	
Artillery Fm	29 · 11 · 17		Considerable Aerial Activity by the Enemy all day. Battalion moved in the evening to Erquinghem – being billeted in ~~the~~ village	

A5834 Wt. W4973/M687 750,000 8/16 D. D. & L. Ltd. Forms/C.2118/13.

Instructions regarding War Diaries and Intelligence Summaries are contained in F. S. Regs., Part II. and the Staff Manual respectively. Title pages will be prepared in manuscript.

WAR DIARY
or
INTELLIGENCE SUMMARY.

(*Erase heading not required.*)

Army Form C. 2118.

Place	Date	Hour	Summary of Events and Information	Remarks and references to Appendices
Erquinhem	30.11.17		Nothing of interest to report. Considerable time spent in arranging billets etc. Weather dull & inclined to rain.	
~~do.~~	~~31.11.17~~			

J Edwards Major
Comdg 1st RWF

A5834 Wt. W4973/M687 750,000 8/16 D. D. & L. Ltd. Forms/C.2118/13.

Vol 24

15th BATT. ROYAL WELSH FUSILIERS

WAR DIARY

FOR

DECEMBER 1917

3

2HD
8 sheets

Instructions regarding War Diaries and Intelligence Summaries are contained in F. S. Regs., Part II. and the Staff Manual respectively. Title pages will be prepared in manuscript.

WAR DIARY
or
INTELLIGENCE SUMMARY.
(Erase heading not required.)

Army Form C. 2118.

Place	Date	Hour	Summary of Events and Information	Remarks and references to Appendices
L W 121			No24.	
			WAR DIARY FOR DEC. 1917	
			15th Bn Royal Welsh Fus.	
			R H Montgomery Lt Col Cmdg 15th R.W.F.	

A5834 Wt. W4973/M687 750,000 8/16 D. D. & L. Ltd. Forms/C.2118/13.

Army Form C. 2118.

Instructions regarding War Diaries and Intelligence Summaries are contained in F. S. Regs., Part II. and the Staff Manual respectively. Title pages will be prepared in manuscript.

WAR DIARY
or
INTELLIGENCE SUMMARY.

(Erase heading not required.)

Place	Date	Hour	Summary of Events and Information	Remarks and references to Appendices
ERQUINGHEM	1 XII 17		nothing of interest to report Weather cold + windy	
do	2 XII 17		Sunday Church parades Football in the afternoon Fine but cold.	
FRONT LINE	3 XII 17		The Bn relieved the 14th Bn RWF in the front line Right Sub Sector. BHQ take up new position in vicinity of SHAFTESBURY House Accommodation short Weather fine but cold	
do	4 XII 17		Considerable aerial activity by the enemy Otherwise all quiet Weather very cold + frosty	
do	5 XII 17		Bn sector shelled with 77 mm + 4.2s in the morning Aeroplanes of both sides very active all day Observation balloons up in large numbers. The enemy let loose small red balloons which dropped leaflets during the afternoon. Weather cold + fine	
do	6 XII 17		Three casualties caused during the morning by enemy TM's Artillery fairly active all day registration Weather cold + fine visibility very good	
do + SUPPORT LINE	7 XII 17		Considerable artillery activity [illegible] TM's fired during the morning. Our guns retaliated Some aerial activity. Relieved by the 14th Bn RWF in the front line + we moved into support positions in the SUBSID[illegible] LINE Weather fine	

A5834 Wt. W4973/M687 750,000 8/16 D. D. & L. Ltd. Forms/C.2118/13.

Instructions regarding War Diaries and Intelligence Summaries are contained in F. S. Regs., Part II. and the Staff Manual respectively. Title pages will be prepared in manuscript.

WAR DIARY
or
INTELLIGENCE SUMMARY.

(*Erase heading not required.*)

Army Form C. 2118.

Place	Date	Hour	Summary of Events and Information	Remarks and references to Appendices
SUPPORT LINE	8 XII 17		Nothing of interest to report. A very quiet day. Weather dull + wet	
do	9 XII 17		Considerable artillery + TM activity all day on whole of Front line system. Weather dull visibility poor.	
do	10 XII 17		Support + rear lines shelled by the enemy throughout the day. Aerial activity increased. Heavy trench mortars fired on our posts at intervals all day. Weather dull.	
FRONT LINE	11 XII 17		At 6 am the enemy opened a heavy barrage on all four lines under cover of which a party of the enemy entered our trenches between PATRICK + PAN posts + found no one in occupation. The raiding party retired leaving behind bombs, equipment etc. Roads + billets behind the front raided were also shelled but little damage was done. The rest of the day was very quiet. Weather cold + misty. The 15th Bn R.I.R. relieved the 14th Bn R.I.R. in the front line at night. Relief complete 7.15pm.	
FRONT LINE	12 XII 17		TM activity at periods throughout the day. Increased aerial activity although visibility was low + weather dull.	
do.	13 XII 17		Early in the morning five 4.2s fell in vicinity of BHQ causing no damage. The same was fired at at about 7pm. Roads used by ration limbers were shelled during the evening.	

A5834 Wt. W4973/M687 750,000 8/16 D. D. & L. Ltd. Forms/C.2118/13.

Instructions regarding War Diaries and Intelligence Summaries are contained in F. S. Regs., Part II. and the Staff Manual respectively. Title pages will be prepared in manuscript.

WAR DIARY
or
INTELLIGENCE SUMMARY.
(Erase heading not required.)

Army Form C. 2118.

Place	Date	Hour	Summary of Events and Information	Remarks and references to Appendices
FRONT LINE	14.XII.17		Our artillery fired during the morning. Situation otherwise quiet. Weather dull + wet	
ERQUINGHEM	15.XII.17		Only normal activity. The 14th Bn relieved the 15th Bn Rif? in the front line + the latter proceeded to ERQUINGHEM. Weather cold + misty	
do	16.XII.17		Church parades in the afternoon. Nothing further to record. Weather cold + heavy frost	
do	17.XII.17		Baths at Bac St Maur in the morning. Inter Coy football contests in the afternoon. Bn concert at the Arena in the evening. Weather cold + some snow	
do	18.XII.17		Parades during the morning. Holiday in afternoon. Weather still cold + frosty	
do	19.XII.17		Parades in the morning. Nothing else to report. Weather very cold	
do	20.XII.17		Owing to new arrangement Bn did not relieve the 14th Bn ~~today~~ yesterday, but relief took place this evening. During the day all stores were moved down to the Transport Lines from ERQUINGHEM as the Australian Corps took over the village + left Sub Sector. Relief complete 7.30pm. Weather cold with hard frost	

A5834 Wt. W4973/M687 750,000 8/16 D. D. & L. Ltd. Forms/C.2118/13.

Instructions regarding War Diaries and Intelligence Summaries are contained in F. S. Regs., Part II. and the Staff Manual respectively. Title pages will be prepared in manuscript.

WAR DIARY
or
INTELLIGENCE SUMMARY.

(Erase heading not required.)

Army Form C. 2118.

Place	Date	Hour	Summary of Events and Information	Remarks and references to Appendices
FRONT LINE	21 XII 17		During the early hours of the morning a patrol of 2 off + 10 O.R. from A Coy left our trenches to examine the enemy wire. Owing to the bright moon light the patrol was spotted + fired on by the enemy. The party withdrew to our lines + it was discovered that one of the officers 2/Lt Newman was missing. A search party was formed to go out and look for him but this party failed to find any trace of the missing officer. It is assumed that he was hit + wounded + taken in by the enemy	
do	22 XII 17		Very quiet today. Owing to mist + low visibility, guns were quiet + TMs did not open. Weather still very cold + frosty	
do	23 XII 17		Increased activity generally. Artillery, both hostile + our own fired a few rounds during the day, + aeroplanes were busy. About 12.0 pm a Boche plane was brought down just behind the enemy front line trench. Night quiet. No change in the weather	
do	24 XII 17		Visibility very bad + in consequence little activity was shown. A few rounds were fired by our 18 prs about 5 pm. Weather warmer	
do	25 XII 17		Christmas Day dinners were served in the trenches + thoroughly enjoyed by all. No activity on our sector, but guns on the right + left were active during the morning. Gifts from England were distributed during the afternoon in very cold weather	

A5834 Wt. W4973/M687 750,000 8/16 D. D. & L. Ltd. Forms/C.2118/13.

Instructions regarding War Diaries and Intelligence Summaries are contained in F. S. Regs., Part II. and the Staff Manual respectively. Title pages will be prepared in manuscript.

WAR DIARY
or
INTELLIGENCE SUMMARY.
(Erase heading not required.)

Army Form C. 2118.

Place	Date	Hour	Summary of Events and Information	Remarks and references to Appendices
FRONT LINE	26 XII 17		The enemy began shelling a battery position close to BHQ at 10 am & continued till 6.15 pm in the evening. Other targets were engaged. Otherwise all was quiet in the line. Weather colder with some [illegible] & snow.	
do	27 XII 17		A quiet day. Nothing to record. Weather cold but slightly warmer.	
do	28 XII 17		A few rounds from a hostile battery on the support line during the morning & artillery activity was [illegible] for the day. We were relieved by the 13th Bn. RWF in the Right Subsector at 7.15 pm & moved to relieve the 14th RWF in the centre Sub sector. Relief complete [illegible].	
do	29 XII 17		Very little activity all day. Weather still very cold.	
do	30 XII 17		The following officers were mentioned in despatches. Lt Col C C Norman, Major Evan Davies, Capt & QM E.J. F. [illegible] (Actg Lt Col) R H Montgomery & 42092 Pte W Richardson	
do	31 XII 17		A very quiet day. Nothing of interest to report. Weather fine but cold.	R H Montgomery Lt Col Cmdg 15th RWF

A5834 Wt. W4973/M687 750,000 8/16 D. D. & L. Ltd. Forms/C.2118/13.

15th BATT. ROYAL WELSH FUSILIERS

Vol 25

WAR DIARY

FOR

JANUARY. 1918.

Army Form C. 2118.

Instructions regarding War Diaries and Intelligence Summaries are contained in F. S. Regs., Part II. and the Staff Manual respectively. Title pages will be prepared in manuscript.

WAR DIARY
or
INTELLIGENCE SUMMARY.
(Erase heading not required.)

Place	Date	Hour	Summary of Events and Information	Remarks and references to Appendices
			No 25.	
			WAR DIARY	
			FOR JANUARY 1918	
			15th Batt. RWF.	

A6945 Wt. W11422/M1160 350,000 12/16 D. D. & L. Forms/C./2118/14.

Instructions regarding War Diaries and Intelligence Summaries are contained in F. S. Regs., Part II. and the Staff Manual respectively. Title pages will be prepared in manuscript.

WAR DIARY
or
INTELLIGENCE SUMMARY.
(Erase heading not required.)

Army Form C. 2118.

Place	Date	Hour	Summary of Events and Information	Remarks and references to Appendices
Bois Grenier (Left Subsection)	January		Slight shelling during the morning by the enemy with 77 mm gun on our subbat lines. Considerable machine-gun activity during the night. Weather very cold. Hard frost	
	1st		14 RWF. relieve the Bn in the line. relief complete by 7.45 PM. Great difficulty was experienced during the relief in getting along the roads — which were exceptionally hard & slippery on account of the frost. The transport finding it almost impossible to control the mules etc.	
Fleurbaix	2nd		The Bn in billets in, and around Fleurbaix, Erquinghem. Bath in the morning at Bac St Maur. Large working parties provided for cable-laying work. Weather extreme cold	
	3rd		The 3rd Jan was set aside as a general holiday for the Batt. in consequence of having spent Xmas Day in the trenches. Concert in the evening at Bac St Maur much enjoyed by the men.	
	4th		Usual RE fatigues to-day. weather still very cold	

A5834 Wt. W4973/M687 750,000 8/16 D. D. & L. Ltd. Forms/C.2118/13.

Army Form C. 2118.

Instructions regarding War Diaries and Intelligence Summaries are contained in F. S. Regs., Part II. and the Staff Manual respectively. Title pages will be prepared in manuscript.

WAR DIARY
or
INTELLIGENCE SUMMARY.
(Erase heading not required.)

Place	Date	Hour	Summary of Events and Information	Remarks and references to Appendices
Fleurbaix	5th		Bn relieve the 13th RIF in the Centre Subsection (Bois Grenier) in the Evening.	
Bois Grenier	6th		Considerable aerial activity during the day. Our Artillery fairly lively. Weather slightly warmer toward night. Some rain.	
do	7th		The Enemy displayed considerable TM activity during the afternoon. & Evening. Occasional bursts of fire by our Artillery in retaliation. Weather much warmer.	
do	8th		Very little activity of any sort. Snow again fell this morning.	
do	9th		Morning very quiet. In the afternoon. however the Enemy 'mortared' our lines very heavily – Weather extremely cold. heavy frost. North wind.	
do	10th		Very little activity of any sort during the day. other than the usual Aerial activity – very dark night Weather windy – but warmer	

A5834 Wt. W4973/M687 750,000 8/16 D. D. & L. Ltd. Forms/C.2118/13.

Instructions regarding War Diaries and Intelligence Summaries are contained in F. S. Regs., Part II. and the Staff Manual respectively. Title pages will be prepared in manuscript.

WAR DIARY
or
INTELLIGENCE SUMMARY.

(*Erase heading not required.*)

Army Form C. 2118.

Place	Date	Hour	Summary of Events and Information	Remarks and references to Appendices
Bois Grenier (Centre)	11th	3.45 AM	At about 3.45 AM the Enemy opened out with TMs and some artillery on our lines with great intensity. Under cover of the barrage, a party of the Enemy attempted to enter our line at 'Pester Post'. The raiding party, about 30 in number, succeeded in getting up to our wire, and in throwing into our trench about 30 or 40 stick bombs. Owing to the gallantry of Sgt Norman Davie.- (NCO in charge of the post) in organising the defense, the attack completely broke down.- We sustained no casualties, it is believed that there were casualties among the Germans. The party left a rifle, two service caps, and a number of stick-bombs in our possession. Sgt Davie was awarded the Military Medal for his conduct during the raid. Our Artillery + TMs were active in retaliation. All was quiet at 4.30 AM. Our Artillery + TMs were active during the remainder of the day. The Enemy again mortared our lines in the evening. Considerable machine-gun fire during the night. Weather cold.	

A5834 Wt. W4973/M687 750,000 8/16 D. D. & L. Ltd. Forms/C2118/13.

Instructions regarding War Diaries and Intelligence Summaries are contained in F. S. Regs., Part II. and the Staff Manual respectively. Title pages will be prepared in manuscript.

WAR DIARY
or
INTELLIGENCE SUMMARY.
(Erase heading not required.)

Army Form C. 2118.

Place	Date	Hour	Summary of Events and Information	Remarks and references to Appendices
Bois Grenier	12th		Activity normal. Weather unchanged.	
do	13th		Nothing to report. Weather unchanged	
do	14th		Snow fell again this morning. Weather colder. Bn was relieved in the line by the 7th East Surrey Regt.. The 38th (Welsh) Division being relieved by the 12th Division. The Bn ~~paraded under~~ arrived at their billets in Sailly-sur-le Lys. at about 12.30 AM Jany 15th.	
Sailly	15th	10AM	The Bn paraded under Bde Arrangements at 10AM to march to Le Sart near Merville, a distance of some 12 Kilos. Rain fell during the greater part of the march. Few men, however, fell out. Bn arrived at	
Le Sart		2.30 PM	Le Sart at about 2.30PM. Some difficulty was experienced in finding billets owing to some hitch in the arrangements. Weather very wet. Some thunder.	
do.	16th.		The day was spent in 'cleaning up' etc. Weather wet & windy.	

A5834 Wt. W4973/M687 750,000 8/16 D. D. & L. Ltd. Forms/C.2118/13.

Instructions regarding War Diaries and Intelligence Summaries are contained in F. S. Regs., Part II. and the Staff Manual respectively. Title pages will be prepared in manuscript.

WAR DIARY
or
INTELLIGENCE SUMMARY.

(Erase heading not required.)

Army Form C. 2118.

Place	Date	Hour	Summary of Events and Information	Remarks and references to Appendices
Le Sart	17th.		Training Programme somewhat upset owing to the rain Usual parades. – Weather wet.	
	18th.		Usual parades. Weather slightly better – no rain.	
	19th		Usual parade. & fatigues. Weather unchanged	
	20th		Sunday. Church parade in the morning. Weather still unsettled	
	21st		Usual parades & fatigues. Weather unchanged.	
	22		Same as yesterday. The evening of the 22 Jan. was set aside as the occasion on which to hold the Bn Xmas Dinner. Which was a complete success. & very much enjoyed by all.	
	23rd		Nothing to report. Usual training. etc	
	24th		Weather bright & sunny. Usual parades.	
	25th		'A' Coy fire at the range. which the Bn had helped to construct during the previous ten days. Weather cooler and misty.	

A5834 Wt. W4973/M687 750,000 8/16 D. D. & L. Ltd. Forms/C.2118/13.

Instructions regarding War Diaries and Intelligence Summaries are contained in F. S. Regs., Part II. and the Staff Manual respectively. Title pages will be prepared in manuscript.

WAR DIARY
or
INTELLIGENCE SUMMARY.
(Erase heading not required.)

Army Form C. 2118.

Place	Date	Hour	Summary of Events and Information	Remarks and references to Appendices
Le Sart	26th		Usual routine. Weather unchanged.	
	27th		Church parades in the morning weather much cooler and very misty in the morning.	
	28th		Nothing to report. Slight frost this morning. Bright & sunny later.	
	29th		Frost continues. Usual parades	
	30th		Frost heavier. usual parades & fatigues.	
	31st		Weather unchanged. 'C' Coy proceed as 'advance party' for work on rifle range & to the new area. — The Bn will follow on Feb 1st. Otherwise nothing to report.	

R H Montgomery Lt Col
Comdg 15th RWF.

A5834 Wt. W4973/M687 750,000 8/16 D. D. & L. Ltd. Forms/C.2118/13.

Vol 26

WAR DIARY

15TH BATTN. ROYAL WELSH FUSILIERS

FEBRUARY 1918

Instructions regarding War Diaries and Intelligence Summaries are contained in F. S. Regs., Part II. and the Staff Manual respectively. Title pages will be prepared in manuscript.

WAR DIARY
or
INTELLIGENCE SUMMARY.
(Erase heading not required.)

Army Form C. 2118.

Place	Date	Hour	Summary of Events and Information	Remarks and references to Appendices
			War Diary for February 1916.	
			15th Batt. Royal Welsh Fusiliers.	
				W. MacDougall Capt. & Adj. 15th R.W.F.

2353 Wt. W2544/1454 700,000 5/15 D. D. & L. A.D.S.S./Forms/C. 2118.

Instructions regarding War Diaries and Intelligence Summaries are contained in F. S. Regs., Part II. and the Staff Manual respectively. Title pages will be prepared in manuscript.

WAR DIARY
or
INTELLIGENCE SUMMARY.

(Erase heading not required.)

Army Form C. 2118.

Place	Date	Hour	Summary of Events and Information	Remarks and references to Appendices
	1918			
Le Sart	Feby 1.		Battalion marched from the Le Sart Area and were billeted for the night in Guarbecque. Weather dull but fine.	
Guarbecque	Feby 2		Battalion marched to Hely [?] in the St Hilaire Area and were all settled in billets before dusk. Weather fine.	
Hely [?]	Feby 3		Usual Church Parades were held. Companies held sports in the afternoon. Weather fine.	
Hely [?]	Feby 4.		Training parades of Musketry, Physical training &c were held in the morning. Companies held Sports in the afternoon. Brigadier General Commanding visited the battalion in the morning. Weather bright and sunny.	
Hely [?]	Feby 5		Parades and Sports were held as yesterday. G.O.C. Division visited the battalion during the parades in the morning. Weather fine.	

2353 Wt. W2544/1454 700,000 5/15 D. D. & L. A.D.S.S./Forms/C. 2118.

WAR DIARY
or
INTELLIGENCE SUMMARY.

(Erase heading not required.)

Army Form C. 2118.

Instructions regarding War Diaries and Intelligence Summaries are contained in F. S. Regs., Part II. and the Staff Manual respectively. Title pages will be prepared in manuscript.

Place	Date	Hour	Summary of Events and Information	Remarks and references to Appendices
Rhyl	1915 July 6		To-day saw the first part of the disbanding of the battalion which had been ordered by authority of Army Headquarters. 5 Officers and 150 O.Rs from each of the Companies were transferred to the battalions as under —	
			A Company to 17th Royal Welsh Fusiliers	
			B do to 16th do	
			C do to 14th do	
			D do to 13th do	
			The battalion paraded on the square at Rhyl and were wished "God Speed" by their old comrades. Lt Col. H.H. Montgomery and Major J. Edwards made very fitting speeches and wished all [illegible] the best of luck wherever they found themselves. Weather hot, dull and windy.	
Rhyl	July 7		The surplus of the battalion spent the day cleaning up the billets. Weather dull but fine.	

2353 Wt. W2544/1454 700,000 5/15 D. D. & L. A.D.S.S./Forms/C. 2118.

WAR DIARY
or
INTELLIGENCE SUMMARY.
(Erase heading not required.)

Army Form C. 2118.

Instructions regarding War Diaries and Intelligence Summaries are contained in F. S. Regs., Part II. and the Staff Manual respectively. Title pages will be prepared in manuscript.

Place	Date	Hour	Summary of Events and Information	Remarks and references to Appendices
[illegible]	1916 July 8		The Fusiliers marched to billets in Amont Fontes. Weather fine but later wet.	
Amont Fontes	July 9.		The Battalion had baths at Auchy-au-Bois, and spent the day cleaning up. Weather dull.	
Amont Fontes	July 10		Baths as yesterday. Weather fine but dull.	
Amont Fontes	July 11		Parades - Drill, Musketry &c - were held in the morning and afternoon. Weather fine.	
Amont Fontes	July 12		Parades as yesterday were held. Weather dull.	
Amont Fontes	July 13		Battalion marched with the Brigade and were billeted in Guarbecque. Weather was very wet.	

2353 Wt. W2544/1454 700,000 5/15 D. D. & L. A.D.S.S./Forms/C. 2118.

Instructions regarding War Diaries and Intelligence Summaries are contained in F. S. Regs., Part II. and the Staff Manual respectively. Title pages will be prepared in manuscript.

WAR DIARY
or
INTELLIGENCE SUMMARY.
(Erase heading not required.)

Army Form C. 2118.

Place	Date	Hour	Summary of Events and Information	Remarks and references to Appendices
	1918			
Guarbecque	Feby 14		Battalion marched to the Neuf Berquin Area and was billeted in Blaffelle Durelle for the night. Weather fine but dull.	
Blaffelle Durelle	Feby 15		Battalion marched with Brigade to Estaires where they left the column and marched to [illegible] Maison west of Steenwerck and was billeted there. Weather fine but dull.	
Steenwerck	Feby 16		Cleaning up of Equipment. C.O. inspection of Bn. Weather bright and sunny.	
do	Feby 17		Battalion found a working party in the Sailly Area. Work consisting of digging a trench for burying a telephone cable. Weather fine.	
do	Feby 18		Working party as yesterday in the Sailly Area. Weather fine.	
do	Feby 19		Working party as yesterday in the Estaires Area. Weather fine.	

2353 Wt. W2544/1454 700,000 5/15 D. D. & L. A.D.S.S./Forms/C. 2118.

Instructions regarding War Diaries and Intelligence Summaries are contained in F. S. Regs., Part II. and the Staff Manual respectively. Title pages will be prepared in manuscript.

WAR DIARY
or
INTELLIGENCE SUMMARY.
(*Erase heading not required.*)

Army Form C. 2118.

Place	Date	Hour	Summary of Events and Information	Remarks and references to Appendices
	1918			
Steenwerck	July 20		Working party as yesterday in the [illegible] Area. Weather fine	
do	July 21		Working party as yesterday in the Bois des Vaches Area. Weather dull but fine.	
do	July 22		Working party as yesterday in the Bois des Vaches Area. Weather fine.	
do	July 23		Working party as yesterday in the Erquinghem Area. Weather fine	
do	July 24		Battalion went to Pont de Nieppe for baths. Weather fine	
do	July 25		Working party as the 23rd in the Erquinghem Area. Weather wet and windy	
do	July 26		Battalion marched to Hallebecque Camp and was put under orders of O.C. No. 1 Entrenching Battalion. Weather fine	
do	July 27		Battalion was this day formed into D Company of No. 1 Entrenching Battalion under the command of Capt. W. Macdonald. Weather fine	
do	July 28.		Battalion was engaged on cable burying under orders of O.C. No. 1 Entrenching Battalion. Weather fine.	W. Macdonald Capt. O.C. 15 Regt. details.

2353 Wt. W3544/1454 700,000 5/15 D. D. & L. A.D.S.S./Forms/C. 2118.

www.ingramcontent.com/pod-product-compliance
Lightning Source LLC
Chambersburg PA
CBHW081355160426
43192CB00013B/2412
* 9 7 8 1 4 7 4 5 1 8 7 1 0 *